WHITE GLOVES and COLLARDS

a memoir

WHITE GLOVES and COLLARDS

a memoir

helen pruden kaufmann

Published by HPK Publishing

Cover and Interior Book Design by Monkey C Media
www.monkeycmedia.com

Cover painting by Carroll Lassiter, native of Edenton, North Carolina
www.frankisart.com

Edited by Lisa Wolff

Printed in the United States of America

ISBN: 978-0-9898011-0-2

Library of Congress cataloging information pending

To Ginny, Chris, and Paul

At home with my mother, 1958.

AUTHOR'S NOTE

This is my story of personal loss and social awakening. It stems from a desire to share childhood memories (both happy and painful) and my interest in our country's racial history. Written from the perspective of a younger me experiencing events as they happened, it's not a typical civil rights era morality tale where heroes and villains are clearly delineated. Rather, it's the story of everyday people dealing with change the best they know how. For some, that meant opening hearts and minds. For others, it was clinging to a myth-filled past. And for most of us, it was doing a little bit of both.

The descriptions and dialogs are based entirely upon my own recollections. While all of the characters are real, I've changed the names of some of them to protect privacy or in some cases, because I can't remember the actual names.

Helen Pruden Kaufmann
Fall 2013

CONTENTS

PROLOGUE

Return to Hallowed Ground

October 1983

Traveling at a cruising altitude of 25,000 feet, I couldn't see the shift in landscape below me—the concrete expanse of the Eastern Seaboard now interspersed with fields of green and yellow, the haze that had clung so tightly to city skylines replaced by cotton-like clouds over gentler sprawl. We'd crossed the Mason-Dixon Line, which a hundred years after being surveyed to settle a property dispute would come to represent the cultural and political boundary between North and South, and then a hundred or so years after that, separate me from the life I'd been born into and the life that I chose.

But even if I'd had a window seat, I probably wouldn't have noticed the scenery. My mind was elsewhere. I had my hands full. All that mattered to me at that moment in time was the child I held in my arms.

As soon as we entered the terminal, I spotted them—Bill standing tall and lean, his kind blue eyes scanning the crowd for us; Mae there beside him with matching shoes and handbag; the two of them still holding hands after nearly fifty years of marriage.

"Well, this must be little Christopher!" Mae cooed while lifting my two-month-old from his infant carrier and holding him close. He'd screamed nonstop since the descent into Norfolk, causing the passengers around me to glare and making me feel helpless as a mother. But once in his great-aunt's arms, he immediately calmed down. "It sure is good to see you!" Bill drawled, his soft-spoken voice as warm and welcoming as ever.

"You both look fit as a fiddle," I said as I embraced the two of them. "You must be giving that dime a good workout!"

Back when I was a teenager, I'd shared with them a *Seventeen Magazine* fitness tip about walking with an imaginary dime squeezed between your butt cheeks, and they'd been joking about it ever since. "Not a day goes by when I don't think about that dime," Bill chuckled. "I carry it with me every time I go out walkin'."

As though it had been only weeks, not a year, since my last visit, we continued our good-natured banter all the way to Edenton, North Carolina—a nearly eighty-mile drive south, mainly on two-lane country roads through swampland, pine forests, and low-lying farmland dotted by modest homes and trailers. With Christopher asleep in his infant carrier and Bill maintaining a steady speed of fifty miles per hour (except when passing the occasional slow-moving tractor), Mae and I chitchatted about my life in New England and caught up on family news. Then, as we crossed the Chowan County line, we turned to the latest developments in Edenton.

"You wouldn't believe the number of new houses being built along the Albemarle Sound," Bill said. "Each one bigger than the last!"

"It's all those northerners coming down here with their retirement money and bad taste," chimed in Mae.

"Watch it!" I shouted with mock indignation. As my aunt and uncle well knew, I'd not only been living and working in the Boston area for the past ten years, I'd also married a native.

"Well, Paul's not like most of 'em," Mae responded, turning toward the backseat so she could give me a wink. "As far as we're concerned, he's just a good ol' boy."

"He sure ate like a good ol' boy," I laughed, referring to the dinner she'd cooked for us when I'd brought him with me the previous visit. He'd endeared himself by devouring her crispy fried chicken and then having seconds of the Sock-it-to-me Pound Cake she'd made from a recipe clipped from the *Chowan Herald*. "He's sorry he couldn't be here for some more of your home cooking."

"We're sorry too," Bill said kindly, "but a man's gotta earn a livin'."

I attempted to describe for him Paul's demanding new job with a computer company, even though I wasn't quite sure myself what a high-tech financial analyst actually did. As I spoke, I gazed out the car window at the county's October-ripe fields of peanuts and cotton, stretching from farmhouse to farmhouse. Then all of a sudden, in what was once a peanut field emerged Edenton's brand-new strip mall—complete with fast-food restaurants, a discount shoe store, and a supermarket. "I now do all my shopping out here at Food Lion," Mae said as we passed it, "'cause the nigras have taken over the S&W Market down the road from us."

I cringed at her word choice and instinctively covered my

young son's ears. "Well, it must be nice to have a McDonald's nearby," I said to change the subject. "Have you tried their new McChicken sandwich?"

"We've only been there for dessert," Mae replied. As she began describing the delicious hot apple pies she and Bill had enjoyed just the other day, I was glad I'd avoided her usual complaints about the residents of the federally funded, low-income housing project on the edge of her all-white neighborhood.

Instead of turning right onto U.S. 17, the quickest way to my aunt and uncle's home, we continued south on Broad toward the waterfront and the heart of town. "Might as well take the scenic route," Bill said, slowing down to a crawl so I could take in the familiar surroundings—the charming, two-block business district lined by turn-of-the-century storefronts; the brick-paved Monument Plaza with its Revolutionary War cannon and memorial to the Confederate dead; and at the end of the street, the cypress-dotted Albemarle Sound, extending into the horizon and sparkling in the late afternoon light.

"I sure did grow up in a beautiful place," I said, more as a statement of fact than with any sort of wistfulness. At least in this part of town, nature and history had prevailed over shopping centers. So much had been preserved over the years—the scenic waterfront, which due to the shallowness of the bay had never become a commercial port; the tree-lined, grid-like street patterns laid out in colonial times; and centuries-old architecture on just about every corner. Each structure offered its own lesson in history. The Georgian-style Chowan County Courthouse was built in 1767, when Edenton was the seat of the royal colony. The white clapboard Visitor's Center was once the home of Penelope

Barker, organizer of a protest by colonial ladies against the British Tea Tax. And many of the graceful antebellum homes on King Street had been in the same families since before the Civil War. No wonder that *Travel and Leisure* magazine recently dubbed Edenton as "the South's prettiest small town."

After circling the Courthouse Green with its terraced lawn and stately sycamores, we left the historic district and finally made our way west on Highway 17 past the Tastee-Freeze and S&W Market toward Mae and Bill's cozy brick home, about a mile outside of town. Unlike nearby properties that had been subdivided into housing tracts with tiny fenced-in yards, the two-acre, grassy lot still extended from the highway to Pembroke Creek with the house halfway between—unchanged since its 1948 construction, except for the conversion of the attic into two pine-paneled bedrooms when my cousins were young and the recent addition of an aluminum carport and toolshed off the kitchen, which blocked the view of the creek.

"Did you bring your rock collection with you?" Bill joked as he lifted my overpacked suitcase from the trunk of his Chevy Blazer. It was the same joke he made whenever I came for a visit. "I brought extra rocks this time," I laughed, "just to make sure you're staying in shape during retirement."

Once inside, I was greeted by the combined odors of Pine-Sol and country ham, a familiar scent that instantly made me feel at home. "Let us know if you need anything!" Mae yelled from the bottom of the staircase as I carried my waking son to the room I'd once called my own. "Not a thing!" I replied, noticing that the accent I'd tried to lose over the years was already reemerging, something it tended to do whenever I traveled south.

I slowly took a seat in the gooseneck rocker next to the old crib Bill had put up in the corner. Then, before Christopher's barely audible whimpers escalated into full-scale wails, I lifted my sweater, undid the snap of my nursing bra, and held my hungry infant close. Unlike so many of my new-mother friends, who no matter where they were brazenly whipped out their breasts at the first sign of fussiness, I was much more private with my feedings—retreating to a ladies' room stall if we were out in public or savoring those quiet one-on-one moments at home. When Christopher began screaming on the airplane, I'd offered him a breast in hopes of quieting him down. But he wasn't hungry; and as I fumbled with the American Airlines blanket I'd draped over my shoulders, he only screamed louder, for I'd nearly suffocated him in my clumsy attempt to cover my bareness.

Now we were both much more relaxed; and as we rocked back and forth, him latched onto me like he'd never let go, I gazed down at the tiny miracle before me. Until giving birth, I hadn't thought I was the mothering type. Now I couldn't imagine a life without him. I'd never before felt so complete—just holding him close could bring tears of joy. And never before in the past sixteen years had I missed my own mother so.

For more than half my life I'd gotten along fine without her, finishing high school, earning a degree from Carolina, and having a successful advertising career. But now I longed to have her near—to hold her grandchild, to know my husband, to tell me I was a good mother. There was so much I wanted to ask her. Had she, like me, been surprised and awed by motherhood? Did she love Norfleet and me as much as I loved Christopher? Before the trip, I'd gone through family photo albums, looking for answers, but all I'd found were black-and-white images of what appeared to be happy times. As much as I wanted to feel her presence in them, I couldn't. As hard as I tried to remember her touch and the sound of her voice, nothing would come. My memories of her had become as distant and two-dimensional as the old photographs. I'd hoped that a trip back to Edenton would spark some sort of reconnection.

As I pondered all those things, Christopher let out a tiny hiccup and then drifted off to sleep. So I slowly rose from the rocker and made my way to the well-worn crib—the same crib Mama had borrowed when Norfleet and I were babies. As I laid my son down and tucked the blanket around him, I tried to picture her doing the same for me. She'd be wearing one of the pastel shirtwaists that showed off her curvy figure. Her face would be glowing. Her touch would be sure.

Of course it was imagination, not actual memory, that brought the scene to mind. But just envisioning the two of us together made me smile. Maybe the time had come for me to let myself remember.

SCENES FROM A SOUTHERN CHILDHOOD

(1956–1965)

1. Pink and Red

I was only five years old when Daddy got sick, old enough to know he had a sore throat, which was why Vanzula served him milk toast for lunch rather than the chicken or beef the rest of us ate, but far too young to understand the meaning of cancer. As far as I could tell, Daddy's illness was no worse than chicken pox, measles, or mumps—diseases I'd already become familiar with in kindergarten. Except for the sore throat, he seemed just fine. No spots, no rashes, no swollen jowls. Just weekly overnight trips to Durham for radiation treatments at Duke Hospital, about a four-hour drive from Edenton. And since Mama always went with him, she'd leave my brother and me with our great-aunt Mag.

Of all the relatives we could stay with, Mag was clearly the best choice. Unlike Mama's sister Mae, who had a family of her own to tend to, Mag was a spinster with plenty of time on her hands. Unlike Mawmaw and Granddaddy, whose house was far out in the country, Mag lived in town, just a few blocks north of us.

And unlike Daddy's sister, Lina, and my grandmother Madam, who also lived nearby, Mag had a car and a driver's license—and although she was seventy-three years old and her vision was failing, she could still see well enough to drive Norfleet and me back and forth to Edenton Elementary.

Her house was a rambling Victorian she'd inherited from my great-grandfather W. D. Pruden, a Civil War veteran and one of Edenton's most prominent citizens. Since she was his only surviving child, she had the entire place to herself—except, of course, for her maid, Lucy, who did all the cooking and cleaning, and Red the yardman, who came twice a week to mow the lawn and clip the hedges. With its huge wraparound porch, high-ceilinged rooms, and countless nooks and crannies, it was the kind of house that could be either intimidating or intriguing—and for my brother and me, it was only intriguing. Nothing about that house intimidated us, not even the creaky back staircases or the cobweb-filled attic with its musty trunks full of moth-eaten hats, china-headed dolls, and *National Geographic* magazines dating back to the early 1900s.

During those overnight stays, Norfleet and I would spend the afternoon hours playing indoor games of hide-and-seek, often discovering new hiding places like the tiny closet of a bathroom next to the servants' quarters, or sometimes going outdoors to play under the giant gingko tree and to explore Mag's small clapboard garage, originally designed for a horse and buggy and barely big enough for her brand-new 1956 Chevy.

By the time five thirty rolled around, the aromas of baking pies or frying chicken would draw us into the kitchen, where Norfleet did his homework while I helped Lucy roll out biscuits for the evening meal. With its black-and-white linoleum floor, dingy white appliances, and tired green walls, the room was far more utilitarian than cozy. If not for the smell of food and Lucy's cheery disposition, it wouldn't have been a very inviting place to go.

"I was just waiting for my little helper to come in and give me a hand," Lucy would always say while wrapping one of her starched white aprons around me, folding the skirt in half and securing it with the sash so it wouldn't drag on the floor. Then as gospel music blared from Mag's old Motorola, we'd flour the dough together and cut out 1½-inch circles with juice glasses, all the while Lucy singing along to the radio—tunes like "His Eye Is on the Sparrow" and "Nobody Knows the Trouble I've Seen." She sounded to me a lot like the gospel singer Mahalia Jackson, who'd recently appeared on *The Ed Sullivan Show*. Except for the gray-and-white maid's uniform, she looked a lot like Mahalia, too.

Eventually dinner would be ready, and I'd remove the apron and wash my hands with reluctance—not because I wasn't hungry, but because I dreaded having to sit politely at the well-appointed dining room table for what seemed like an eternity. Mag firmly believed that conversation was as important a part of the meal as food. So without our parents there to talk to, she'd try to engage Norfleet and me in discussions about the upcoming presidential election or the threat of communism or the sanctity of states' rights. I'd just sit there squirming in my seat, silently waiting to be excused. But Norfleet, who was in third grade and old enough to read the *Weekly Reader*, knew enough about current events to keep the conversation going. The only thing I knew was that Mag had some strong opinions—she absolutely adored the Democratic candidate Adlai Stevenson and couldn't stand a Supreme Court judge named Earl Warren. "He and that court of his have no business telling us how to treat our coloreds," she once said as Lucy quietly cleared the table.

Mag also had strong opinions about my brother and me. In her estimation, we were born to do great things. Every A on Norfleet's report card was a sign of genius. Each one of my stick-figured kindergarten drawings was a masterpiece. In her eyes, we were model children who could do no wrong—which is why I was so stunned the day she accused me of going to school without my underwear.

It was a Wednesday morning, and I was sitting cross-legged with my friends on the braided blue rug in the front of the kindergarten classroom as our teacher, Mrs. Ross, read aloud from *Uncle Wiggily's Adventures*. When we heard a gentle tap-tap-tap, Mrs. Ross rose to open the door, and there was tall, skinny Mag—all dressed up in olive-green wool and carrying a foil-wrapped package in one of her white-gloved hands. After a few whispered words, Mrs. Ross beckoned me. Then when my great-aunt and I were left alone in the hallway, Mag unfolded the foil and held up a pair of pale pink underwear embroidered with the word *Wednesday*.

"I just found these in your overnight bag and hurried right over," she said. "You should know better than to go to school without underwear."

I stared at her in disbelief. Of course I was wearing underwear! It was the same underwear I'd kept on overnight, and I'd seen no point in changing it. But before I could fully explain, Mag was lifting my skirt and exposing my yellow *Tuesday* pair to anybody who might be walking down the hall.

"Well, as long as you're covered, dear," she said sweetly while lowering my skirt. Then, as if nothing had happened, she rewrapped the *Wednesday* pair, kissed me goodbye on my forehead, and told me she'd see me after school.

I returned to the classroom, my face as red as a beet. And later that night, after Mama and Daddy returned home from Durham, I announced that I would never, never, ever stay with my great-aunt Mag again.

"It doesn't look like you'll have to," Mama said with a sigh. "Your father's had about all the radiation he can handle."

Within a couple of weeks, Daddy was too weak to go to work. Then by the beginning of December, when I turned six, he was spending most of his time in bed. Even milk toast was becoming hard to swallow, so Mama ordered a food processor through the Byrum Hardware on Broad Street. When it arrived three days after Christmas, I went with her to pick it up. On the way home, we stopped at the P&Q Market to buy a pound and a half of calf's liver, which Dr. Williams said would help restore Daddy's strength.

Later that afternoon, I watched from the kitchen table as Mama cut up and floured the dark, shiny slab and placed it in a hot frying pan along with some bacon and onions. As the fat sizzled, a surprisingly pleasant odor filled the room. When it was done, Mama began spooning a portion into the food processor just as the hall telephone rang.

"I'll let you get that," she said, knowing I liked to practice my telephone manners: *Pruden residence, this is Helen speaking, may I ask who's calling?*

It was Nurse Simpson, letting us know that Dr. Williams had just left the office and was on his way to our house for his daily check on Daddy.

"Perfect timing!" Mama said as she pressed one of the food processor buttons, creating a noise that was so loud we both had to cover our ears. Soon the crispy brown liver was transformed into a grayish-tan pudding, and I was about to say that it was the most disgusting thing I'd ever seen, when we heard my brother scream from the rear of the house. "Mama, come quick!" he cried. "Daddy's spitting up blood!"

Mama rushed into the hallway, me at her heels. When Daddy appeared before us with a blood-soaked handkerchief over his mouth, she quickly guided him into the hall bathroom. "Go outside and wait for Dr. Williams!" she shouted to my brother and me.

Within minutes the doctor's dark green Buick pulled into the driveway, and as Norfleet rushed out to greet it, I hurried back inside to tell my mother. But when I reached the bathroom doorway, I couldn't speak, for the scene before me was so horrifying that it took my breath away. Blood, bright red blood, was everywhere—dripping from the toilet seat and splattered all over the pink linoleum floor. Daddy, who was seated in the white cane chair next to the toilet, looked up, but he didn't seem to notice me. Mama, who was standing behind him, said to me in a voice that was eerily calm, "Go wait with your brother in the living room."

When I sat next to Norfleet on the living room sofa, I was trembling. "Is Daddy gonna be okay?" I asked, reaching for his hand.

He paused for a moment, for he was trembling too. "As long as he can get a blood transfusion," he finally said, sounding not quite as confident as he usually did when answering my questions. Then he began to describe an episode he'd just seen on *Dragnet* where a man was bleeding to death from a gunshot wound but an ambulance came and took him to the hospital, where the doctors removed the bullet and gave him fresh, new blood. By the end of the program, the man was good as new.

The story calmed me, and when the ambulance arrived a few minutes later, I knew that Daddy would get the help he needed—just like the man on *Dragnet*. But then Mama entered the room, and before I could tell her what I knew about blood transfusions, she said in a voice that was so soft it was almost a whisper, "He's gone." She wasn't crying, but the expression on her face was so strange and forlorn that I ran to her and hugged her as tightly as I could, hoping I could squeeze away all the sadness. Norfleet joined us, and the three of us just stood there in the middle of the living room clinging to each other for I don't know how long until Mag arrived to take Norfleet and me to her house for the night.

The only other thing I remember about that evening was sitting at Mag's dining room table, where for once there was no talk of Adlai Stevenson or communism or states' rights. We hardly spoke at all. And as Mag half-heartedly picked at her hamburger (or beef patty, as she liked to call it), I was glad I wasn't eating that God-awful liver.

When Norfleet and I woke up the next morning in Mag's twin-bedded guest room, Mama was stretched out in the corner chaise lounge. She smiled at the sight of us, and as she rose to her feet, she told us that she loved us and that everything would be okay. She bent over to kiss me, and for a brief moment I believed that things would change—that she'd now have more time to spend with me. But of course she wouldn't, for there were mourners to greet and funeral arrangements to be made. "I'm going to have you and Norfleet stay here for another night or two," she said. "It'll be better for all of us."

Since she considered me far too young to experience the rituals associated with death, Mama arranged for me to have a play date with my friend Martha Jean on the day of the funeral. I really didn't mind, for I'd gotten tired of having to spend so much time with my brother, who'd be going to the service with Mama and Mag. Plus, Martha Jean had just gotten a brand-new pair of roller skates for Christmas, and she'd said that I could try them out.

They were much faster than the hand-me-down skates I'd inherited from my cousin Ann, and soon after Mama dropped me off that morning, I was gliding around the Pembroke Circle pavement, pretending I was Carol Heiss on ice. It was during my third lap that I came up with a great idea. *Maybe I'll ask Santa Claus to bring me new skates for Christmas next year!*

After we'd skated until we could skate no more, we played with Martha Jean's dolls, and then helped her mother make sugar cookies, and then had a tea party—and I didn't even think once about Daddy being dead or about people gathering at Beaver Hill Cemetery to put his body to rest.

But later that day, when Mama and Norfleet picked me up to finally return home and begin our life as a threesome, I could feel a tightening in my stomach. I wondered if that God-awful, tan-gray liver was still on the kitchen stove—or if Daddy's bright red blood still covered the bathroom floor.

As soon as we entered the house, I could see that the kitchen had been tidied, but I was afraid to go anywhere near the hall bathroom. I avoided it for days. Then one morning before school, when Norfleet was taking his own sweet time in the other bathroom, I had to pee so bad that I couldn't wait a minute longer. Holding my crotch, I hurried down the hallway toward the room where I'd last seen my father. When I reached the doorway, I hesitated and then slowly peered inside. The toilet was spotless. The pink floor shimmered. All traces of red were gone.

2. The Caregivers

Sometimes I think I missed Vanzula more than I missed Daddy. Not that I loved her more; I just knew her better. It was she and Mama who tended to my daily needs. Daddy was simply the provider. He was the kind of father who'd get to know me later, when I was older. But he never got the chance.

I have only one memory of just Daddy and me together. He'd come home early for lunch one day and taken a seat in the living room, where I was busy playing with my paper dolls. "So what do you have there, Little Sister?" he asked, looking down at the cardboard figures and paper dresses I'd carefully lined up on the carpet.

"The Lennon Sisters," I replied as I hopped into his lap to introduce the dolls one by one.

"Howdy do, so pleased to meet you," he said to each of them. Then he repeated their names—Dianne, Peggy, Kathy, and Janet—

so he wouldn't forget them. If he hadn't gotten sick with cancer, he might have gotten to know *all* my paper dolls.

Vanzula, on the other hand, knew my entire collection by heart because she was the one who cut out their clothes while we watched *Love of Life* during the hour before lunch. It was part of the daily routine we'd established when Mama started helping Daddy in his law office a few mornings a week—that along with trips to the P&Q Market.

Hand-in-hand, we'd head up Broad Street, Vanzula in her gray-and-white maid's uniform and me swinging my child-sized red patent-leather purse. Inside it would be the few extra coins Mama often left with the grocery money so I could buy a new paper-doll book from Rose's Five and Dime.

Once done with our shopping, we'd usually make a stop at the Belk Tyler's department store so Vanzula could use the restroom before returning home. "I'll be just a few minutes," she'd say, and I'd stand outside the door labeled *Colored Women* while she tended to her business. Most days she was done before I knew it. But then she started taking much longer—and I began to wonder if she was in there smoking a cigarette, as my mother did each morning while sitting on the toilet, or maybe reading the newspaper, like my father. One day I decided to investigate.

Ever so quietly, I opened the heavy metal door and sneaked inside. The small, tiled room was almost identical to the store's restroom for white women, where I'd once gone with my mother. There was a sink, a mirror, and a separate toilet stall. Below the stall's partition, I could see Vanzula's white lace-up shoes, her thick, dark ankles, and the P&Q grocery bag next to her feet. Without making a sound, I squatted low for a peek, expecting Vanzula to be seated on the toilet. But instead, she was standing tall and drinking from a pale green bottle. I couldn't quite tell what it was, but I had a feeling she was doing something she wasn't supposed to do. So I quickly rose to my feet and sneaked out as quietly as I'd entered.

I waited until bedtime to tell Mama about what I'd seen. When I was done talking, she scrunched up her face, something she did when she was angry, and for a minute I thought she was mad at me for sneaking into the colored women's restroom. "Damn that Vanzula," she finally said. "She told me she was on the wagon."

From that day on, there were no more shopping trips with Vanzula to the P&Q, Rose's, or anywhere else for that matter—which really didn't bother me too much because summer soon arrived and Norfleet, who'd just finished second grade, was now available to play with me all morning. But then toward the end of August, just before I entered kindergarten, Vanzula suddenly stopped coming to work.

"It was time for her to retire," Mama said when I asked her about it. And that was that. There'd been no goodbyes, no parting hugs, no keeping in touch. Vanzula, who'd spent as much time with me as my own mother, was simply gone—just like Daddy would be four months later.

Left with funeral expenses, medical bills, and two children to raise on her own, Mama got a job as a teller at the People's Bank & Trust, only a block from our house, and hired a woman named Maggie to tend to my brother and me after school.

"Can I fix you a little snack to tide you over till lunchtime?" Maggie would ask each morning when I was dropped off after my half day of kindergarten.

"I'm not hungry," I'd reply.

"Then let me cut out some paper-doll dresses for you," she'd offer.

"No, thanks. They've already been cut out."

"Well, how about a little TV? It's almost time for *Love of Life*."

"I don't like that show anymore."

I really didn't have anything against Maggie—she was only trying to please. But she wasn't Vanzula, and without Vanzula there to look after me, I only wanted to be with my mother. So as soon as I changed out of my school clothes, I'd hurry across the yard to the little historical park at the foot of Broad. I'd climb on top of the Revolutionary War cannon that was mounted on a slab of concrete. And there I'd sit for the next hour or so, until Mama came home for lunch.

As the minutes ticked away, I'd gaze up Broad Street—just like the Confederate soldier statue in front of me, him facing north with defiance, me looking toward People's Bank with longing. I'd be so intent on my mother's return that I'd hardly notice the cold winter winds blowing off Edenton Bay, or once spring arrived, the intense midday heat that radiated off the cast-iron cannon.

Eventually the clock in the center of town would strike one, and I'd stand up tall on the cannon's rounded barrel, all the while craning my neck and struggling to keep my balance. Then when Mama's tall, slender figure appeared in the distance—all dressed up in high heels and a pastel shirtwaist that swished when she walked, I'd leap to the ground and run to her as fast as I could. "I'm so hungry, I could eat a horse!" she'd say while lifting me into her arms.

And I'd say, "I'm so hungry, I could eat a whale!"

Maggie didn't last long. By the time school got out for summer, Mama had replaced her with a woman named Helen Austin, and we all thought it was funny that our household now had three Helens—my mother (whose first name was Helen), Helen Austin, and me, Little Helen.

Unlike Maggie and Vanzula, who were heavy and dark, Helen was young and slender, had skin the color of butterscotch, and wore a skirt and blouse to work rather than a maid's uniform. (She also used the pink-linoleum hall bathroom instead of the colored women's restroom at Belk's.) Mama liked the fact that she was a teetotaling Baptist, which meant there'd be no worries about the grocery money going toward Thunderbird wine. And Norfleet and I liked the fact that she was quiet and just let us be—as long as we didn't leave a mess.

As far as Helen was concerned, her job was to keep the house in order, not to be our servant. If we wanted a snack, she'd say, "Fix it yourselves." If we told her we were bored, she'd just roll her eyes. And if we got into a fight, she'd refuse to intervene, even when it was completely obvious I was the victim—like the time when Norfleet called me Petunia Pig for eating the last Eskimo Pie.

"I'm not Petunia Pig!" I snapped, for I was sensitive about my lingering baby fat and didn't like being compared to Porky's chubby girlfriend.

"Petunia Pig! Petunia Pig!" he taunted. And with that, I did what I always did when I lost my temper. I stormed into my bedroom, slammed the door, and began crying as loudly as I could. Helen, of course, was too busy keeping the house tidy to pay me any mind. So as I worked myself up into a lather, I was left with only one choice—to sustain my tears and anger until Mama came home for lunch so she'd see my misery and reprimand Norfleet for calling me names.

And there I was, lying on my bed, sobbing and feeling sorry for myself, when I heard a faint rumble in the adjacent hallway. I lifted my head just as dozens of marbles rolled through the space beneath the bottom of the door and the hardwood floor—bright blue peewees, black shooters, and yellow cat's-eyes. From what I could tell, I was being invaded by Norfleet's entire marble collection.

I angrily rose from the bed and made my way toward the door, careful not to trip over the tiny spheres ricocheting around me. Then as I opened it, I couldn't believe my eyes. Right there before me was a magnificent chute, constructed from the hard-bound biographies Norfleet received in the mail each month as a member of the Landmark Book Club. Stacked end-to-end and aslant, the pastel volumes formed a ramp that extended all the way from the hallway bookshelf to the doorway of my room.

"What in the Sam Hill?" I shouted, suddenly more intrigued than angry.

"I made a marble machine," Norfleet answered proudly and invited me to play.

For the next hour or so, we rolled marbles down the colorful raceway, pitting shooters against peewees, cat's-eyes against swirls, agates against steelies—all the while marveling at the way gravity guided each ball down its own course. When Helen eventually appeared before us with hands on hips, I'd completely forgotten about my earlier rage.

"You two chil'ren better clean up this mess," Helen said sternly, obviously not as impressed by Norfleet's invention as I was. "Your mama's gonna be home for lunch in just a few minutes."

"Yes'm," we replied in unison, for we didn't have a choice. Vanzula would have let us keep the structure intact, and Maggie probably would have cleaned it up herself. But Helen was Helen, and we knew she meant business. So we gathered the marbles and returned the Landmark biographies to the shelf, finishing the job just as our mother entered the front door.

"My goodness!" Mama exclaimed after she'd hugged us. "It's so nice to come home to a clean and tidy house!" Then she turned toward Helen and said, as though *she* deserved all the credit, "I don't think I could manage without you."

3. An Unlikely Playmate

I was in the den watching *Captain Kangaroo* when the young, dark girl appeared before me—tiny braids sticking out all over her head and wearing a pink, puff-sleeved dress that was more appropriate for Sunday school than a weekday morning in June. "Hello," she said shyly. "Hello," I mumbled back. Then as she took a seat on the edge of the sofa, I tried to pretend she wasn't there.

Her presence wasn't unexpected, for Mama had gotten a call from Helen Austin the night before asking for the day off to visit her husband, a sailor, who'd just been granted a twenty-four-hour shore leave in Norfolk. "And bless her heart," Mama said after hanging up the phone. "She's arranged for her mother to be here in her place."

Helen had been working for us part-time for over a year now, and the thought of somebody new made me scowl. "There's no need to worry," Mama assured me. "Rosa's real nice. Plus she'll be bringing her younger daughter, Georgia. She's about your age. You'll enjoy the company."

I could hardly believe my ears. No one had ever told me explicitly, but I knew there were certain rules about black and white children playing together. Up until a certain age, it was fine to play outdoors on neutral turf, as Norfleet and I sometimes did with Snoddy and Donnie Mae, two children who lived on Black Cat Alley down by the docks. But visiting each other's homes was simply not done.

"But she's colored!" I cried.

"I know she's colored," Mama replied, "but it's too late for me to make other arrangements, and Rosa can't leave Georgia alone. We'll just have to make the best of things." Then she looked me straight in the eye and said, "I'll leave it up to you to decide whether or not you want to play with her, but I expect you to at least be nice." And with that, she pursed her lips and firmly nodded her head, which was her usual way of telling me, "And I mean it."

So there we were, Georgia and me at opposite ends of the sofa, neither of us saying a word as Bunny Rabbit, Mr. Green Jeans, and Captain Kangaroo moved about the TV screen.

"Do you want to go outside and play on the swing set?" Georgia asked when the show was over.

"No!" I snapped. Then, remembering what Mama had said about being nice, I added, "We can't go outside because it's too hot." But the real reason was that I didn't want any of my friends from school to ride by and see me playing with a colored girl right there in my own front yard.

For the next hour or so, we continued to watch TV—a rerun of *I Love Lucy*, followed by *December Bride*. We were halfway through *The Garry Moore Show* when Norfleet entered the room with a Chutes and Ladders board game in hand. "Wanna play?" he asked cheerfully. Georgia said she didn't know how, so he explained the rules to her. Since I had nothing better to do, I joined them on the back porch.

When Mama arrived home for her lunch hour, Norfleet and I sat down with her at the dining room table while Georgia disappeared into the kitchen. "How was your morning?" Mama asked as Rosa served us our meal.

Norfleet told her about our games, pointing out that Georgia had beaten me twice at Chutes and Ladders. Then he wolfed down his lunch so he could make it to Little League practice on time. That's when Mama turned to me and asked all matter-of-factly, as though Georgia was just another friend from school, "So what are you girls going to do this afternoon?"

What I really wanted to do was ignore Georgia altogether and watch *As the World Turns* and *Art Linkletter's House Party* all by myself, but I didn't want to disappoint my mother—especially since she'd just praised Norfleet for teaching Georgia our games. "We're gonna play with my paper dolls," I replied.

So while Rosa washed the lunch dishes, I laid out my cardboard collection on the living room floor as Georgia looked on with interest. Under each doll, I carefully lined up the appropriate costumes (most of which had been cut out a couple of years earlier by Vanzula). Then as I demonstrated how to bend the little white tabs to make the clothes fit, Georgia suddenly reached for Elizabeth Taylor's slinky red evening gown and placed it right on top of the

Roy Rogers cutout. At first, I was angry that she'd do something so outrageous, but then I imagined the real Roy Rogers dressed up like Elizabeth Taylor and giggled. When I reached for Shirley Temple's blue-and-white sailor dress and placed it on Dale Evans, Georgia giggled too. Before I knew it, we had Queen Elizabeth wearing Fred Astaire's top hat, Ava Gardner all dressed up for a rodeo, Gower Champion in Marge's ballroom dance outfit—and we were both laughing so hard I didn't even think about the fact that Georgia was colored. "C'mon," I said after we'd put together every possible combination. "Let's go outside and play!"

As we swung back and forth on the front-yard swing set, I was now curious about this funny, dark girl who was spending the day with me. "How old are you?" I asked while pumping my legs to go higher and higher.

"Seven, going on eight."

"Then where do you go to school?" I asked next, realizing she was just a little older than me, but certainly not a student at Edenton Elementary.

"I go to D. F. Walker," she replied in midair. "It's the colored school."

"Well, what do you want to be when you grow up?"

"Maybe a majorette or a cheerleader."

"Me, too!" I shouted.

With that, the two of us leapt to the ground and began marching up and down the front sidewalk, first as majorettes, using sticks as our make-believe batons—and then as cheerleaders, Georgia rooting for the D. F. Walker Hornets and me shouting "Go, Aces, go!" just like the John A. Holmes High cheerleaders who led parades up Broad Street before Friday night football games.

We were still marching and shouting when Mama arrived home from work at a quarter past four. "Looks like you girls are having a good time," she said while giving me a peck on the cheek.

The three of us entered the house together, and as Mama reached into her purse for cash and thanked Rosa for filling in for the day, Rosa turned to her daughter and asked, "What do you have to say to Little Helen?"

"Thank you, Little Helen," Georgia said softly, and I smiled at the way her voice sang rather than spoke the name adults used when addressing me.

"You're most certainly welcome," I replied, trying to sound like a gracious hostess.

At dinner that night, Georgia was all I could talk about—how smart she was and how we both wanted to become majorettes or cheerleaders. Then as my mother tucked me in at bedtime, I asked if Georgia could come back for another play date.

Mama became real quiet for a moment, as though carefully considering my request. "I don't think so, Sweetie," she finally said. "Today was a special situation because both Rosa and I were in a bind. For now at least, I think it's better for you to stick with your friends from school."

"Yes, ma'am," I replied sadly—sort of understanding, but not really.

Mama leaned over and kissed me. Then instead of saying "good night, sleep tight, don't let the bedbugs bite" as she usually did when tucking me in, she settled down on the edge of the bed and told me a story about when she was a little girl.

During the long, hot summers, Mama began, she and my uncles would sometimes visit the children of a sharecropper who lived on a neighboring farm. In the dusty front yard of the tiny, unpainted shack, they'd play games of tag, red rover, and tug-of-war—never going inside and always keeping an ear out for the sound of my grandmother's farm bell, which meant it was time to come home for lunch or dinner. "Living so far out in the country, we couldn't get together with our friends from school," Mama explained. "It was nice to have some children nearby to play with, even though they were colored."

One afternoon in late August while her brothers, Rupert and Willie, were helping with a harvest and her little sister, Mae, napped, my mother walked over to the shack on her own, taking a shortcut through the pine copse that separated the two properties. The front yard was empty—probably because the sharecroppers' children were at work in the fields. She was about to head back home when the aroma of boiling collards wafted toward her and lured her up the rickety front-porch steps to the open doorway. Inside the dark, sparsely furnished room, she could see the children's grandmother crouched over a wood-burning stove and stirring a large, cast-iron pot. When the old, toothless woman invited her in for a bowlful, she couldn't resist. "I've never in my life tasted better collards!" Mama exclaimed as she described for me the dark green leaves, cooked to a mush, floating in a fatty brine known as pot liquor, and so infused with the smoky flavor of ham hocks that you hardly knew you were eating vegetables.

Late that afternoon, when Rupert and Willie returned from the fields, she told them about the delicious treat they'd missed out on, hoping to make them jealous. But my grandfather overheard the conversation and after a bit of shouting and cursing, demanded that she go outside and break off a switch from the hickory tree. "It's the only time he ever beat me," Mama said quietly. "He told me it was just plain wrong for a white girl to sit at a colored person's table." She winced as she spoke, as though she could still feel the sting of the lashes.

It was hard for me to envision my grandfather cursing or beating anyone—I knew him only as the kind, gentle man who spoke in a whisper due to cancer surgery before I was born. I wanted to ask questions like "Why was Granddaddy so angry?" or "Where did he hit you?" or "Did you cry?" But before I could speak, Mama turned off the light, gave me another kiss, and headed to the den to watch *The Wednesday Night Fights* with my brother.

Left alone in the dark, I contemplated the story I'd just heard. Whenever my mother talked about her childhood, there was always some sort of lesson involved, like "Make do with what you've got" or "Appreciate the value of a dollar." Her stories usually centered on the Great Depression, not collards and beatings. So what was she trying to teach me now? And what did it have to do with Georgia and me?

At age seven, I was just beginning to understand the intricacies of black-white relations—what you could or could not do, where you could or could not go, when to be friendly, when to keep your distance. Under the Jim Crow system that still lingered, there were so many innuendos, contradictions, and illogical rules to grasp. It was sort of like learning an unspoken language or a series of complex dance steps that eventually become so natural that you don't have to think about them. As I snuggled under my covers, I wondered if Mama, through her story, was reminding me of those rules. Or perhaps she was lamenting their absurdity.

I'd learn over time that it was a little bit of both.

Norfleet and me on vacation.

4. Nags Head

It seemed like Mama was always working—eight hours a day, six days a week, fifty weeks a year—except for Thanksgiving, Christmas, and New Year's, as well as bank holidays like Veteran's Day and George Washington's Birthday, when she'd go to Norfolk with Mag and my aunt Lina for the sales at Smith & Welton. Unlike other mothers in town, she had little time for cookie-baking, afternoon soap operas, or constant watch over her children. Not even in July, when People's Bank & Trust gave her two weeks off for our annual vacation at Nags Head.

We'd begin the nearly ninety-mile car trip like any normal family, telling knock-knock jokes and singing "Ninety-nine Bottles of Beer on the Wall" while heading east toward the Outer Banks along low-country roads and bridges. Halfway there, we'd stop at a roadside farm stand, where Mama liked to stock up on fruits and vegetables and treat Norfleet and me to snow cones. "I didn't realize I had two purple-tongued children," she'd joke after we sucked the last few drops of fruit-flavored syrup from the wilted paper cones—and it would feel so good to have her right there with us in the middle of a weekday afternoon. But we'd eventually reach my great-aunt's beachfront cottage with the waiting cars in the driveway, and I'd know that family time was about to end. At least for the next five days or so, mother and children would be having our separate vacation fun.

Since Mag and her maid, Lucy, never arrived until the second week of our stay, Mama often invited friends from Edenton to fill the empty rooms—usually one or two couples her own age whose children were already grown. "It's a good way to repay my social debts," she'd explain. But it seemed to me that she was more than compensating for the few times she'd been invited over for late afternoon drinks because if you were an adult at Nags Head, each day was one big cocktail party.

During the hours before lunch and dinner, Mama and her Bermuda-shorts-clad houseguests would join the dozens of other adults who gathered on one of the rambling porches that lined the Atlantic shore—porches connected to gable-roofed, brown- or gray-shingled, two-story cottages like the one Mag had purchased during the 1920s from money she'd made in the stock market. Nicknamed "the unpainted aristocracy," these turn-of-the-century summer homes represented some of North Carolina's oldest and most prominent families, most of them returning summer after summer, generation after generation. Surrounded by sand and facing the ocean, they were built atop wooden pilings so they could be easily moved inland as the hungry sea encroached. It was in that resulting three-to-four-foot space between the porch and the cool, shaded sand where Norfleet and I liked to play.

As the grown-ups chatted and sipped bourbon above us, we'd be invisible to them, creating our own little vacation world. Often other invisible children joined us, and together we'd build miniature cities of sand, collect seashells, and dig for live sand fiddlers. Sometimes we'd leave our sheltered hideout to play "capture the flag" in the nearby dunes or make our way to the ocean's edge, where we'd frolic together in the salty air, relishing the freedom of childhood. But eventually hunger would set in, and I'd look toward the porch and the reveling adults (some of them now teetering down the steps) and hope that Mama would soon realize that it was time to go back to the cottage and make us lunch or dinner.

Once Mama's friends were gone and Mag and Lucy arrived for the remainder of our vacation, the days became more orderly—breakfast at eight, lunch at one, and dinner at six thirty sharp. Unlike the party-going houseguests, the two seemed glad to be around us children—Mag going out of her way to include us in mealtime conversations, and Lucy always laughing and joking when we'd watch her cook and clean.

Just by looking at them, you'd think they were still in Edenton. Lucy, of course, was there for work, not vacation, so it wasn't surprising that she'd wear only her gray-and-white maid's uniform—even during her time off, when she'd visit other maids in the servants' quarters of other cottages. But Mag, who'd never put on a pair of pants or a swimsuit in her entire seventy-plus years, got dressed each morning in stockings, sensible heels, glasses that hung from a chain around her neck, and a blue or green linen shirtwaist that hung from her skinny frame. She'd spend the mornings in her favorite porch rocker, reading the newspapers that Norfleet and I picked up at Kessinger's General Store across the road—not just the *Raleigh News & Observer*, but the *Virginian Pilot* and the previous day's *New York Times* as well. "Even when on vacation, it's important to keep up with current events," she'd say while peering over her pale, tortoise-shell reading glasses.

Instead of Mag attending cocktail parties on the neighboring porches, the neighbors came to her. ("Your great-aunt likes to hold court," Mama would joke as one by one or in groups of two or three, they came to pay their respects.) All kinds of people stopped by—important ones like Reverend Drane, who preached at Saint-Andrews-by-the-Sea across the highway, and Dr. Frank Porter Graham, a former U.S. senator who'd been president of Carolina. Then sometimes there'd be a visit from a man named Jack, who scared the living bejeezus out of me.

Born with severe deformities and a respected Edenton name, he'd taken up residence at Nags Head after the death of his parents. I had no idea where he stayed at night, but he spent his days drinking beer in the back of Kessinger's. Norfleet and I would see him when we picked up Mag's newspapers, and I'd always look the other way, pretending he wasn't there.

When he'd come staggering up Mag's sand-covered driveway, I'd cringe at the sight of him—his pigeon-toed feet stepping on top of each other as though his legs were connected at the knee, one arm bent at the elbow, making his hand flap close to his face, and a mouth so distorted it practically hung below his unshaven chin. Before he could see me staring at him, I'd scurry into the cottage.

Mag and Mama always greeted him warmly, as though he were Reverend Drane or Dr. Graham. Then as the three of them sipped cocktails from one of the porch's protruding benches while engaging in cheerful chatter (even though Jack's slurred speech was hard to understand), Norfleet would come out and say something like "Hello, Mr. Badham, so nice to see you," which was what Mama taught us both to do whenever Mag had visitors.

"Where's your sister?" Mama would ask—and as Norfleet tried to cover for me by saying he didn't know, I'd be making myself small beneath the living room card table. "Little Helen, come out here and say hello to Mr. Badham!" she'd shout, her firm voice inescapable as it shot through the open window. So I'd go out onto the porch, trying not to notice the smell of urine and stale beer, and say, "Hello, Mr. Badham, so nice to see you," just like Mama taught me.

Fortunately, Mag's visitors never stayed long because she'd offer them only one cocktail. "Drinking should be done only in moderation," she liked to say—a policy that suited me just fine because with limited socializing, Mama had more time to spend with my brother and me. She'd take us on morning trips to places like the Wright Brothers Memorial in Kitty Hawk or the Ben Franklin Five and Dime in Manteo, or to souvenir shops along the highway. Except for not having a daddy with us to drive the car and buy us treats, we'd be like any normal family on vacation.

But even with all that family togetherness, Norfleet and I still had plenty of time on our own—especially during the early afternoon, when Mag insisted on peace and quiet. After lunch, she'd retire to her downstairs bedroom for a nap, and Mama, Norfleet, and I would head upstairs to the large, wood-paneled room that overlooked the ocean. Within minutes, Mama would be snoring on her cot as Norfleet and I played quiet games of cards on the bare floor beside her.

One afternoon during a never-ending game of War, Norfleet suggested that we stop playing cards and take a walk to the pier instead. "You're on!" I said, thinking he meant the Nags Head Pier, which was less than a mile away and where we often went at the crack of dawn to see the fishermen bring in their seines. But as we skipped across the hot, dry sand toward the water's edge, he announced that we'd be heading in the opposite direction—to Jennette's Fishing Pier, which was barely visible on the horizon.

"But it's so far!" I shouted above the roar of the surf. "It'll take all day."

"Oh, c'mon!" he shouted back. "It'll be an adventure."

So off we went, weaving in and out of the sea-foamy tide, our bare feet leaving tracks on the sand (his about an inch longer than mine). "I'm getting tired," I complained after a while. We'd been walking for what felt like an eternity, and Jennette's Fishing Pier didn't seem to be getting any closer.

"We can't quit now," he replied. Then as we continued on, me struggling to keep up with his long, determined stride, he began reciting a poem he'd learned at school. It was about snowy woods, which seemed ridiculous to me because it was the middle of July and there wasn't a single tree in sight—only sand and sea, a string of beachside motels, and a barely visible pier in the distance. When he got to the part "but I have promises to keep and miles to go before I sleep," I grimaced.

"Are you sure you want to walk all the way to the pier?" I asked for the umpteenth time. But he just ignored me and kept on reciting. *And miles to go before I sleep. And miles to go before I sleep.*

Nearly one hour later, when we finally arrived at the barnacled pilings of Jennette's Fishing Pier, Norfleet was so jubilant that he held up his fists like one of those prizefighters on TV. As for me, all I could think about was having to turn around and walk all the way back to the cottage. My bare feet ached, my lips were parched, and I was about to complain about how tired and thirsty I was when Norfleet produced a shiny quarter from the pocket of his navy shorts. "Let's go up to the bait shop," he said. "I'll bet they have a soda machine."

We slowly climbed the sandy embankment to the weather-beaten structures that formed an entrance to the 740-foot-long pier. Careful not to step on broken glass or rusty beer cans, I kept my head down until we reached the black asphalt parking lot. Then as I looked up, I saw her in the distance, barreling toward us with car keys in one hand and the light of the late afternoon sun making her salt-and-pepper hair glow like a halo. At first I thought it was an apparition—maybe I'd been out in the heat too long. But then I heard that familiar voice.

"What in the hell do you children think you're doing?" Mama shouted when within earshot. "You know better than to wander off like this! I've been worried sick!" As Norfleet and I ran toward her, all I wanted to do was to reach out and hug her, but I knew that wouldn't be a good idea right in the middle of a tongue-lashing. She grabbed my hand, and as she led us both toward the waiting car, Norfleet asked sheepishly, "How did you know where to find us?"

Mama stopped in her tracks and looked at us. "I know a lot more than you think I do," she replied, her taut upper lip loosening, her glare suddenly turning into a twinkle. "I have eyes in the back of my head."

Norfleet laughed—and although I didn't quite get the joke, I smiled. Just having her near made me feel safe and secure.

5. August Storms

After the initial euphoria of being released from Edenton Elementary for three months, boredom would eventually seep into my childhood summers. With Mama at the bank all day and Helen Austin busy ignoring us, it was up to Norfleet and me to fill the long, hot days on our own. While at first it was exciting to be able to watch TV whenever we wanted, go crabbing in the bay, play games on the back porch, and even walk by ourselves up Broad Street for a Coke or an ice cream cone at Mitchener's Pharmacy, those activities would eventually become repetitive and boring. By the time we returned from July vacation at Nags Head and August rolled around, the freedom we'd so cherished in June was more burdensome than exhilarating. The days would be harder to fill, and we'd actually look forward to the start of a new school year and the structure it would bring.

Eastern North Carolina's oppressive late-summer heat waves didn't help matters. The rising mercury, accompanied by 98 percent humidity, slowed each day to a crawl and inflicted us with a languor that made even the simplest game a chore. A quick dash through the sprinkler might offer some relief, but most days, just sitting in front of the TV set was about all we could manage. Often the air would become so stagnant that the setting sun was no guarantee of a drop in temperature. Those were the evenings when our porch became a gathering place for friends and relatives seeking relief. Only a few feet from the bay, it was as likely a place as any to catch a breeze, and with screens on all sides, it offered protection from the swarms of mosquitoes that congregated at dusk. "Come join us," Mama would say to our guests. "Misery loves company." And there we'd sit until bedtime, fanning ourselves with old issues of *The Saturday Evening Post* and hardly speaking at all. It was just too darn hot for conversation.

After a few days of heat and humidity that approached intolerable, dark clouds would form over the Albemarle Sound in the late afternoon or evening. As the temperature suddenly dropped, the air would begin to stir with a restlessness that was both exhilarating and ominous. Eventually the sky would open up with a vengeance, and from the shelter of our screened-in porch, Norfleet and I liked to watch the drama unfold. Standing close to the edge, we'd dare the rains to make us wet. Then as lightning bolts darted from the heavens to the bay before us, we'd determine their distance by counting out loud until we heard thunder.

"Feels like a storm's coming," Mama said one evening as a gust of wind streamed through the open kitchen window. "Let's hurry up with the dishes so we can go out on the porch to watch."

We'd just finished eating, and I was busy scraping the dinner plates, my nightly chore since turning eight the previous December. "Yes, ma'am!" I replied, and no sooner had the words come out of my mouth when a streak of brilliant yellow light darted past me, missing my head by only inches. Almost simultaneously, a loud boom rattled the kitchen. A giant ball of fire suddenly appeared above the kitchen stove and then disappeared as quickly as it came. By the time I'd leapt from my chair to cling to my mother, the only evidence that lightning had struck was a small puff of smoke and my trembling body.

From that day on, storms were no longer exciting to me; they were downright terrifying. So each night at bedtime, right after asking God to keep Mama healthy and alive, I'd pray, "Please, dear Lord, don't send us any more thunderstorms." But storms, of course, were as inevitable as those hot August days. When the next one struck a few afternoons later, I hurried to my room to try a different prayer. "Dear God," I begged, "please don't let me get struck by lightning."

As I knelt before my bed and repeated my prayer, thunder roaring in the distance, I remembered what Mama had said about the Lord helping those who help themselves. So I rose to my feet, grabbed a towel from the hall linen closet, and wrapped it around my head turban-style to protect myself from any errant lightning bolts. Then I hurried into the living room, took a seat at the spinet piano, and played the last piece in my *John Thompson's Teaching Little Fingers to Play* music book. It was called "From a Wigwam," but I made up my own lyrics:

Storm, storm, please go away!

Storm, storm, please go away!

While lightning flashed above the bay and the rains pelted our closed windows, I repeated the words again and again, louder and louder each time. Between verses, Norfleet told me I was crazy and Helen Austin just rolled her eyes. But I was sure my method was effective, because the storm passed quickly and not one single lightning bolt dared to enter the house.

A few days later, when I'd survived yet another storm, Mama arrived home from work shortly after the rains stopped. "What's this doing here?" she asked when she saw the blue towel I'd left on the piano bench.

"It's my protection against lightning," I said, while demonstrating how I wrapped my head. Then I performed my song.

Mama just laughed when I was done. "That's all very nice," she said, "but you don't need to worry, Little Helen. Lightning never strikes twice at the same place."

"Are you sure?" I asked.

"Absolutely!"

I could feel a weight being lifted from my shoulders—and it wasn't just my fear of storms. If lightning didn't strike twice in the same place, I reasoned, then neither would cancer. I'd no longer have to worry about Mama getting sick and dying like Daddy.

6. The Country Girl

Once upon a time, there was a poor country girl (my mother) who got a job as a secretary at the Edenton Peanut Mill right after high school. The second oldest of four children, she'd graduated at the top of her class with dreams of going to college to become a teacher. But the Great Depression hit, and my grandfather, a small farmer, lost the money he'd put aside for her education. Mama didn't complain—she was lucky to be working. Soon she was earning enough money to rent a room in town, feed and clothe herself, and continue her education on her own by joining the Book-of-the-Month Club, seeing movies at the Taylor Theater, and subscribing to the Sunday New York Times. *Her town-bred high school acquaintances quickly became her closest friends; and before she knew it, she was traveling with them to elegant places like New York and Charleston and attending parties in some of Edenton's finest antebellum homes.*

It would be years before she'd finally cross paths with my father. Almost a decade older than she, he'd been away for a good part of his life—first at prep school in Virginia, followed by college and law school, and then a brief job up north. He'd tried to enlist during World War II, but his feet were too flat to fight. So instead, he returned to Edenton to carry on the family's law practice. That's when he became a fixture in the town's social scene, attending dinner parties, cotillions, and Daughters of the American Revolution teas—usually with his widowed mother, whom he'd nicknamed Madam *because of her demanding ways.*

Despite Madam's domination, Daddy occasionally attended functions alone, and it was at a birthday gathering for a mutual friend when he finally laid eyes on Mama. After so many years in town, she looked nothing like a country girl. Her hair was fashionably bobbed, she wore a blue silk dress from Lord & Taylor, and she carried herself with a certain elegance that complemented her shapely figure. She knew exactly who he was. (He was, after all, one of the town's most eligible bachelors.) And when the two were finally introduced, it was love at first sight for both of them.

The courtship was fast and secretive. Daddy, now in his forties, never truthfully explained to his mother why he was no longer available for her parties and teas. By the time she got wind of the planned elopement, the couple was already preparing to drive to the next county for a civil ceremony and then on to Charleston for the honeymoon. Madam was furious.

She quickly donned her favorite coat (the brown cashmere one with a collar of foxes biting each other's tails) and her white kid gloves. She placed a purple-feathered hat atop her hennaed hair and grabbed her purse. Then off she went on foot toward the Courthouse Green and the house on the edge of it where my mother had rented a room for the past few years. She moved at a steady clip, each step fueled by a determination to prevent what she considered to be a terrible mistake.

As she crossed the grassy expanse, she could see her son's tan ragtop in the boardinghouse driveway. The top was down, and he and Mama were already in the front seat. "Wait!" Madam screamed. "Please wait!" She waved her arms and quickened her gait, but it was too late. By the time she reached the edge of the driveway, the car was gone and all that was left was a trail of dust.

After the honeymoon, the couple settled into the little white house Daddy had bought just before the elopement. Although located on what was then called the "cheap side" of Broad, it had a certain charm about it. A tall weeping willow stood in the front yard, azalea bushes filled the gardens, and a huge screened-in porch on the side of the house was only steps from the Edenton Bay. It was the perfect spot for settling down and raising a family.

During the weeks and months that followed, friends celebrated the marriage with parties and gifts, Mawmaw and Granddaddy welcomed their new son-in-law with Sunday dinner on the farm, and Daddy's aunt Mag (the unmarried sister of his late father) dropped by with a silver tea service that had been in the family for years. But there was a noticeable silence from Madam's house—no gifts, no phone calls, not even an acknowledgment that the wedding had ever taken place.

The silence lasted for the next ten months—until the birth of my brother, James Norfleet Pruden III, named after my father and grandfather. Upon hearing the news, Madam was thrilled that the Pruden name would continue. So as soon as mother and child were released from the hospital, she dropped by with a silver spoon, a cup engraved with the monogram JNP, and an invitation for Saturday night dinner, which would become a weekly tradition.

Of all the family stories I'd hear as a child, that was one of my favorites. It had romance, history, interesting characters—and depending on the teller, it was always evolving with new plot twists, embellishments, and points of view.

In Mama's version, Madam was only a little unkind. "Why didn't she want Daddy to marry you?" I once asked.

"I guess she just wanted him all to herself," Mama replied, offering few details.

But when I asked Mama's sister, Mae, the same question, I got a completely different interpretation. "The problem was that high falootin' families like your father's just didn't mix with country folks like us," she told me. "Your grandma Pruden didn't think your mama was good enough for your daddy."

I couldn't imagine anybody thinking Mama wasn't good enough, but Mae's explanation made a lot of sense to me. Madam *did* have a snooty way about her, always sticking her nose up in the air and acting like she was better than everybody else. But that wasn't why I never liked her, nor was it because she'd once snubbed my mother. My reason was clear and simple: I didn't much care for my grandmother because she never seemed to care much for *me*.

I can't remember her hugging me once—or telling me she was proud of me. Although she'd complain when Norfleet and I spent more time with her sister-in-law Mag than with her, she never acted particularly happy to see us. The most she ever said to me during those weekly Saturday dinners was *Harrumph*—a sound she made when I'd entice Norfleet to play tag during cocktail hour rather than sit politely with the adults, or when I'd fidget at the table as Lillie, the maid, served our meal, or when I'd play "Chopsticks" on the piano after dinner rather than one of the classical tunes I'd learned in piano classes.

If not for my aunt Lina and uncle George, who lived with Madam and were always happy to see me, those Saturday nights would have been unbearable. It also helped that Norfleet agreed with me about our grandmother's haughtiness. When out of earshot, we'd mimic her loud *harrumphs*—and during the ride over, we'd sing "The Madam show is about to begin, the Madam show is about to begin" to the tune of the *Alfred Hitchcock Hour* theme song.

"Now, now, children," Mama would say from the driver's seat. "That's not very nice." But I could tell from her stifled smile that she thought our song was pretty funny. Except for the hennaed hair, Madam *did* look a lot like Alfred Hitchcock—especially the profile.

When it came to visiting relatives, Sundays with Mawmaw and Granddaddy in the country were much more to my liking. Right after services at St. Paul's Episcopal (which Mama joined soon after marrying Daddy), Mama, Norfleet, and I would hurry home to change out of our church clothes, make a quick stop at the drugstore for Mama's pre-ordered Sunday *New York Times,* which had arrived overnight on a Trailways bus, and then head to the farm, about ten miles outside of town. It seemed a lot farther, for we'd have to drive slowly on the bumpy country roads past cotton and peanut fields, white clapboard farmhouses, and weathered sharecropper shacks.

When we'd finally pull into my grandparents' front yard and park under the giant sycamore, often before Mawmaw and Granddaddy returned from services at Yeopim Baptist, Norfleet and I would hop out of the car and dash to the barnyard to greet the animals—many of which we'd given names like Henrietta, Clucky

Lucky, Porky, or Petunia. Then we'd hurry over to the dilapidated shed to play on top of the John Deere tractor or scale the bales of hay that were stacked in the corner or head over to the chicken coop to see if there were any eggs. As far as I was concerned, there was no better place to spend a Sunday afternoon, except for two things—going to the bathroom and eating Sunday lunch.

The house had no indoor plumbing (and no heat either for that matter, just a potbellied stove in the room off the kitchen). Mawmaw kept a chamber pot beneath her side of the bed for nighttime use, but if I needed to relieve myself during the day, it meant going outside and peeing in the woods, as Norfleet and my cousin Henry liked to do, or using the creaky old outhouse that stood behind the chicken coop. I'd do my best to avoid either—especially the outhouse, which was dark and drafty inside and stunk so much it could take your breath away. Norfleet and Henry once locked me up inside until I agreed to reenact with them a scene from *Gunsmoke*, and after that, I vowed I'd never again enter that damp, smelly place, no matter how bad I had to go.

Eating was much harder to avoid, and I dreaded the sound of the outdoor farm bell because it meant I'd have to go inside, sit down at the table, and face platters of fried chicken and smoked country ham. It's not that Mawmaw was a bad cook (she wasn't), but her food came directly from the farm, not the P&Q Market, and I couldn't bear the thought of eating a chicken or hog I might have once known. The cooked vegetables bothered me too, for they'd simmer for hours on top of the woodstove with a slab of fatback, which I knew came from Granddaddy's annual hog killings.

The only parts of the meal I considered fit for my consumption were the dill and half-sour pickles Mawmaw put up each fall.

From what I could tell, they contained only vinegar, alum, salt, a few spices, and cucumbers—and not one single bit of Henrietta, Clucky Lucky, Porky, or Petunia. While the adults raved about the oh-so-tender chicken (whose neck Mawmaw had wrung the day before) or the collards seasoned to perfection, I'd load up my plate with pickles—and as long as I kept busy chewing, no one would notice the uneaten meat and greens I'd shoved to the side.

"Sister, what's wrong with your face?" Norfleet shouted one Sunday as I finished what was probably my tenth pickle. All eyes turned my way, and when I got up and looked at myself in the sideboard mirror, I saw that my lips were double their normal size and about as white as the crocheted tablecloth. "I look like a monster!" I screamed.

Mawmaw quickly rose from the table and led me into the kitchen to give me a glass of water with some baking soda. "This should do the trick!" she said as she instructed me to swish the concoction around in my mouth to neutralize the pickling effects of vinegar. Then she stooped down low so that her wrinkled, sun-spotted face was eye level with mine. "I'm glad you like my pickles, Little Helen," she said with a wink, "but if I were you, I wouldn't make a meal of 'em."

"Yes, ma'am," I replied to my all-knowing grandmother.

If the aunts, uncles, and cousins hadn't joined us for Sunday lunch, they'd usually arrive soon afterward. Then, while the grown-ups gathered on the front porch or around the potbellied stove, depending on the season, the children would head outside to play. During late fall, we'd build forts from the mounds of straw left from the harvesting of peanuts. If it was summer and the corn was at its peak, we'd play hide-and-seek among the stalks. And if there were enough of us, we'd sometimes get the uncles to join us for a game of baseball in the open lot—the perfect diamond, as long as we avoided the sheep droppings.

Sometimes I was the only girl, which usually didn't bother me, but some Sundays I'd get my fill of silly boyish games and go back to the house to join the adults. "Come on over here and give me a little sugar," Mawmaw would say when she saw me, and I'd snuggle up to her on the sofa or porch swing (depending on the season). As the aunts chitchatted and the men dozed off in their chairs, I'd sit there quietly, sometimes gazing at my mother across the way.

Without her clip-on earrings or the "Cherries in the Snow" lipstick she always wore at home, Mama would look nothing like the sophisticated lady who'd dined at Madam's house the night before. Instead of silk and pearls, she'd be wearing a simple plaid shirtwaist. Instead of sipping cocktails and smoking Salems, she'd be sitting straight in her chair with arms crossed in front of her, looking relaxed, but not quite at ease. And unlike at Madam's house, where she'd tell witty stories about my brother and me or share tidbits of gossip she'd heard at the bank, she'd listen more than talk as Mawmaw and the aunts went on and on about recipes, childrearing, and the threat of integration.

When my mother did speak, her voice would sound twangier than normal, and I once heard her say something that took me by surprise. "I ain't saying I always agree with him," she'd said during a conversation about Reverend Martin Luther King, "but you've got to admit he's one smart nigger."

Ain't and *nigger* were words my grandparents and some of the other relatives used often. ("They don't know any better," Mama once explained.) But they weren't words we used at home. "*Ain't* 'ain't' in the dictionary," Mama would joke while correcting my grammar; and when Norfleet once repeated a riddle he'd heard at school, *What's another name for a cocoon? A n-nigger*, she'd hit the ceiling. "I never want to hear you say that word again," she'd scolded. "The proper term is *Negro* or *colored*."

As the discussion of Reverend Martin Luther King continued, I squinted at my mother to show my confusion, but she wouldn't return my gaze. So I waited until we returned home from the farm to question her. "Didn't you tell us that *ain't* and *nigger* weren't proper?" I asked from the kitchen table as she opened a can of Campbell's Alphabet Soup for our supper that night.

She was silent for a moment, seeming both embarrassed and surprised by my question. "You're right, Sweetie," she finally replied. "I shouldn't have used those words. But sometimes adults say things they shouldn't just because they want to fit in."

I was still confused, but said nothing more. Then as she slowly stirred the soup, she turned toward me and sighed. "I'll do my best to never use those words again," she said. "I promise."

At Mag's house for dinner.

Lina and Madam on the Courthouse Green.

Mama's side of the family: Mae, Uncle Willie, Granddaddy, Mawmaw, Mama, and Uncle Rupert.

7. Blue Ridge Blues

I don't know which was worse, my uncle George's snoring or the rusty creak of the springs beneath the thin mattress of my roll-away cot. It was the second and last night in a motel room with my aunt and uncle, and I couldn't sleep—and it wasn't just because of the noise. I missed my mother and was desperately counting the hours before I'd return home to Edenton and be with her again.

The trip had been my aunt Lina's idea. Each August, she and George traveled to the Blue Ridge Mountains for a few days as a respite from my uncle's job as a highway engineer and my aunt's constant care of Madam, who was becoming more and more demanding with age. The previous summer, they'd taken my brother with them to southwestern Virginia, and by all accounts, it was a fabulous trip. Norfleet raved about the Luray Caverns' stalactites and stalagmites. Lina and George, who were both in their sixties and had no children of their own, found it rejuvenating to travel with a young person. This year it was my turn.

Even though I was now almost ten, certainly old enough to spend a few days away from my mother, I'd been reluctant to go. "We'll be taking a tour of Biltmore," Lina said to convince me. "It'll be like visiting a castle. You'll love it!"

And she was right. The tour of the Vanderbilt family's estate was the best part of the trip. Perched atop a hillside overlooking the Blue Ridge Mountains, the 255-room mansion was like something out of a fairy tale. There was a magnificent banquet hall with a table as long as a bowling alley, a mahogany-paneled study with more books than I'd ever seen, and upstairs in Cornelia Vanderbilt's rose and pink bedroom were porcelain dolls and a dollhouse that was almost as grand as the mansion. The tour guide's detailed description of life during the Gilded Age had me so fascinated that for a couple of hours, I almost forgot about how much my aunt was getting on my nerves.

It had started the day before, during the eight-hour car ride that took us from the flat farmland of eastern North Carolina, through piedmont towns like Raleigh and Greensboro, and then on to Asheville and its hilly surroundings. I'd sat quietly in the backseat of the Chevy while George did the all driving and Lina, who'd never gotten a driver's license, did all the talking. Even though she hadn't been in a classroom for more than thirty years, her voice still projected the enthusiasm and authority of a teacher. Florid and shrill in tone and about an octave higher than average, it was the kind of voice that never seemed to tire.

Mile after mile, Lina pontificated about the passing scenery. She reminisced about trips from years before. She commented on the weather. It was all meaningless chatter that could easily be tuned out or ignored, except that interspersed within her high-pitched monologues were questions like "I declare, Little Helen, aren't those the most beautiful loblolly pines you've ever seen?" or "Have you ever been on a highway with so many big trucks?" or "Don't you just love these warm summer days?" They weren't difficult questions, but Lina expected answers. So I'd respond with "Yes, ma'am, they are," or "No, ma'am, I haven't," and occasionally "Yes, ma'am, I do."

By the time we reached the Asheville city limits, my legs were aching from too much sitting and my head throbbed from too much listening. But when we finally pulled into the Howard Johnson's parking lot and I saw the aqua-blue swimming pool beneath the restaurant's "33 Flavors of Ice Cream" sign, I perked up. I'd been in the ocean at Nags Head many a time, but never a motel pool. "Oh, please, please, please," I begged. "Can I go in for a dip?"

At first Lina resisted, for it was already cocktail hour, and she was looking forward to settling into the room and joining my uncle for a "toot" from the silver flask of bourbon he kept beneath the front seat of the Chevy. But she eventually relented, and I soon found myself floating on my back in three-foot-deep water while she and George watched from the nearby lounge chairs. Still in their travel clothes—Lina wearing pearls and a blue-gray linen dress that matched the color of her freshly permed hair, George in a plaid short-sleeved shirt with a tie—they looked out of place next to the swimsuit-clad younger couple who sunbathed while their children played Marco Polo. I was about to join the game. But as I dog-paddled toward the laughing children, I heard my aunt call out to me. "Little Helen," she shrieked in a loud singsong voice that reverberated across the pool, "don't forget to hold your nose when you go underwater!" Suddenly the children's laughter stopped and all eyes turned toward Lina, who was now standing near the pool's edge, arms folded across her ample breasts, looking completely out of place. Overcome with embarrassment, I quickly changed my course and slithered out of the pool.

"Have you already had enough?" Lina asked while handing me a towel.

"Yes, ma'am," I replied quietly. "I sure have."

To my surprise, the first night in the motel room wasn't so bad. Maybe I was exhausted from the long trip, but I went straight to sleep and didn't wake up until the next morning when I heard Lina chirp, "Rise and shine, Little Helen! Rise and shine!"

We hurried off to breakfast, and as I feasted on a stack of Howard Johnson's pancakes, complete with sausages and syrup, my aunt described the day's agenda—a drive along part of the Blue Ridge Parkway, a tour of the Biltmore Estate, and then maybe a stroll through the Asheville Arboretum. Her high-pitched enthusiasm resonated throughout the motel restaurant—and from the corner of my eye, I could see the other diners looking our way, some with amusement, others with a sneer. I quickly gobbled up my last few bites so we could return to the room and prepare for the day.

"Be sure to bring along a sweater," Lina trilled as I sat on the edge of the cot to re-lace my Keds. "You never know about this mountain air." Then, when my uncle left the room to purchase a pack of Camels from the vending machine outside, she sat down next to me and asked in an uncharacteristically quiet voice that was at least an octave below her normal pitch, "Have you had a bowel movement this morning?"

I looked up in disbelief. Nobody, not even my mother, had ever asked me such a thing. "No, ma'am," I replied shakily, which was the wrong answer because for the next hour or so, throughout our drive along the Blue Ridge Parkway, Lina went on and on about the importance of good bowel habits while traveling. She extolled the virtues of prune juice and Raisin Bran. She told me about a trip a few years back when she'd had to take a laxative, and because the Ex-Lax took so long to do its job, she and George had missed a guided tour of the Cherokee Indian Village. As we made our way along the curvy mountain highway, I looked at my uncle, thinking he'd be embarrassed by the subject matter, but he just kept driving and smoking his Camels.

When we finally arrived at the Biltmore visitors' center, Lina and I went off to "powder our noses," and when I emerged from the toilet stall a few minutes later, my aunt was waiting by the sink. "Well, did you have a bowel movement?" she asked anxiously, again in that quiet, octave-below-normal voice.

"Yes, ma'am," I lied. "I sure did."

As I lay awake on the motel cot that final night, I tried to ignore my uncle's snoring and the creaky springs below me. I tried to forget about my aunt's embarrassing questions. I tried not to miss my mother. It was already past midnight, and I'd been tossing and turning since before nine when Lina turned off the lights, saying we needed a good night's sleep so we'd be "bright-eyed and bushy-tailed" for the journey home.

Only a few more hours, I told myself. *Only a few more hours.* By late the following afternoon, I'd be back in Edenton, back to familiar surroundings, back with my mother. I'd be staying up late with her, snuggling on the sofa and watching a rerun of

The Twilight Zone. Then she'd tuck me into bed and say, "Sleep tight, don't let the bed bugs bite," and I'd fall asleep to the comforting sound of her puttering around in the kitchen.

But the problem with homesickness is that it doesn't listen to reason. Sure, there were only a few hours until the next morning and the drive back to Edenton. Sure, I'd be back home with my mother by late afternoon. But right then, right there, each minute seemed like a painful eternity. My body ached from the previous night on the thin mattress. My mind raced with dread of another day with my aunt and her annoying high-pitched voice.

The funny thing was that back in Edenton, I actually *liked* the sound of Lina's voice—how its "you-can-do-no-wrong" chirpiness offset my grandmother's "you-can't-please-me" iciness. During those Saturday night get-togethers, I liked the way she'd belt out show tunes while playing Madam's baby grand after dinner—and how she'd sometimes take me aside during cocktail hour to tell me stories about her horse-and-buggy childhood, or how she'd been among the first coeds to attend the University of North Carolina, or how she'd studied in Paris right after the Great War. I'd relished every detail, and her high-pitched shrillness hadn't bothered me one bit. Mama once told me there are some people who can be taken only in small doses. Maybe Lina was one of them.

I closed my eyes again, but sleep still wouldn't come. The snoring became louder, the cot more uncomfortable, the yearning for my mother more intense. Then I asked myself, *What would Mama do in my situation?* For certain, she wouldn't be lying in bed whining. "Stop your bellyaching!" she'd say to my brother and me when we'd gripe about too much homework or being bored or not liking what she'd fixed for supper. "If you don't like something the way it is, change it—and if you can't change it, make the best of it." Even under the worst circumstances, she had a way of making things tolerable, even funny. Just that past April when I'd come down with the chicken pox and was practically itching to death, she'd daubed calamine lotion on my spots and joked, "Well, at least you're in style—I just read in the *New York Times* fashion section that polka dots are all the rage this season."

I began to imagine arriving home and telling Mama about the trip. She'd probably laugh about the bowel movement questions. And my uncle's snoring? Surely she'd crack a joke—maybe something like, "Well, at least he's making himself heard, 'cause most of the time Lina won't let him get a word in edgewise."

Not bad! I chuckled to myself. And before I knew it, I was drifting off to sleep.

The Confederate Monument.

8. The Sit-in

Cast in bronze, he stands atop a pedestal at the foot of Broad Street, in memoriam to those who fought and died for The Cause—for states' rights and the land they loved. Each day he whispers to the boys and girls walking past him on their way to Edenton Elementary or John A. Holmes High. "Be proud," he tells them. "Be proud of your past. Be confident in the future. This is your *land."*

For another group of children heading toward D. F. Walker on the far side of town, he has a different message. "Be on your guard," he warns. "Don't get uppity. Know your place. I'm watching you." Then as they pass before him, eyes toward the ground, he whispers, "This is not your land. You're only here to serve."

But one bright February morning, some brave, dark children have heard enough. They look up at the soldier's musket, his wide-brimmed hat, and the names of Confederate dead inscribed on the pedestal below. "You're wrong," they say in unison. "This land was built by our ancestors brought here against their will. It's the land of our parents and grandparents. We belong here as much as you." They stare for a moment at those hard, cold eyes. Then with heads held high, they turn away and make their way across the street.

"*Our* coloreds are happy," Mag said soon after we arrived at her house for Friday night dinner. "It's all those outsiders comin' in and stirring things up." What she was referring to was the sit-in that had taken place that very afternoon at the Mitchener's Pharmacy lunch counter—and although she hadn't seen it firsthand, she'd heard about it from her friend Miss Clara Preston, who was picking up a prescription when the arrests were made. "Accordin' to Clara," Mag continued while serving us cocktails (bourbon for Mama, ginger ale for my brother and me), "those young coloreds marched right in and took a seat on the lunch counter stools, just like they owned the place. Can you imagine such a thing?"

I was only a fourth grader at the time and not quite sure what a sit-in was, but the distress in my great-aunt's voice got my attention. From what I'd seen on the TV news, there were problems between the races in places like Alabama and Mississippi, but that all seemed so far removed from peaceful little Edenton. Sure, there were weekly demonstrations in front of the Taylor Theater to protest the rule that non-whites enter through a back alley and sit separately in the cramped, decrepit balcony, but that was easily forgotten once I'd purchased my own movie ticket and was seated among friends in the comfortable seats downstairs. As far as I was concerned, Mag was right—"our coloreds" were happy.

"I'm not a bit surprised by any of this," Mama said as she lit up a Salem. "Since those protests at the Woolworth's in Greensboro last month, sit-ins have been taking place all over the state. I don't see why Edenton should be any different."

"Well, I think it's all very shocking," said Mag.

When Lucy entered the living room to announce that dinner was ready, Mama and Mag suddenly became silent—as though they didn't want her to hear their discussion. Then as we made our way into the dining room, conversation shifted to the upcoming raffle at St. Paul's to raise money for the poor and the tasty beef stew Lucy had fixed for supper. But it wasn't the last I'd hear about the sit-in.

"I hear they slapped a hefty fine on those troublemakers," said my aunt Lina the following evening when we gathered at Madam's house for our usual Saturday night dinner. "Hopefully that'll teach 'em a lesson." According to her and my grandmother, the sit-in was staged by just a few "bad apples"; most of Edenton's black citizens wouldn't even consider doing such a thing, for they appreciated all the white community did for them—all those boxes of hand-me-down clothes donated to maids and their families, the extra cash passed out at Christmas time, the brand-new bookmobile that gave them access to books the whites-only Town Library no longer needed. "Those young folks just don't know how good they've got it here!" exclaimed my aunt. "Harrumph!" said Madam in agreement.

Mama's side of the family didn't think much of the sit-in either, as I'd learn the following afternoon on the farm. "I don't know why they'd even want to eat at Mitchener's," Mawmaw said as she dished out Sunday dinner. "Those niggers have their own lunch counter right there at Coon's Corner."

"If the Lord wanted us to mix, he wouldn't have made us different colors," chimed in an aunt.

"Ain't it the truth!" said another.

It was during the drive home later that afternoon when I decided to weigh in on the matter. "I sure hope there aren't any more sit-ins," I said as we slowly made our way down the bumpy country roads. "I'd hate to have to sit next to a colored person the next time I get a Coke at Mitchener's."

"And what's so bad about sitting next to a colored person?" asked Norfleet from the backseat.

Until the sit-in, it had never occurred to me that blacks *couldn't* sit at the lunch counter, and even after listening to so much adult conversation over the past few days, I was hard pressed to come up with a quick answer. "It's just not sanitary," I finally replied. "We shouldn't be drinking from the same glasses as coloreds."

"Well, doesn't Helen Austin drink from our glasses when she's taking care of us?" Norfleet asked. "Do you think that's unsanitary?"

I turned toward Mama for help, but she just kept on driving, looking straight ahead with her hands on the steering wheel, all the while smiling that funny little stifled grin of hers that told me she was getting a kick out of the conversation.

"W-w-well," I stammered, "that's different because I *know* Helen."

"And do you know all the white people who sit at the Mitchener's lunch counter?" he asked next.

Of course I didn't, but before I could answer, he shifted his line of questioning. "How would you like it if *you* couldn't sit at the lunch counter just because you're a girl?"

"I wouldn't like it one bit!" I snapped. Then I turned up the volume of the car radio to drown out any more questions.

Darn that Norfleet! Why did he always have to make me think so hard?

During the weeks and months that followed, the weekly demonstrations in front of the Taylor Theater continued, but there were no more sit-ins at Mitchener's. Even so, from overheard conversations I got the feeling that Edenton would never be the same. When talking about matters of race, there was a sense of foreboding in the adults' voices—like when a hurricane is making its way across the Albemarle Sound and all you can do is stock up on Vienna sausages and tape up the windows. "I hate to say it," Mag said to my mother one Friday over cocktails, "but integration is inevitable, even right here in Edenton. It's no longer a matter of *if*, but rather of *when*."

Although she never came out and said she supported integration, Mama did have a thing about fairness. When local NAACP activist Golden Frinks was about to bounce a check at the People's Bank & Trust, she gave him a call so he could deposit enough funds to cover it, a courtesy routinely offered to the bank's white customers. Her co-workers had criticized her for helping a troublemaker—I'd heard her talking about it after church one Sunday with our minister, Mr. Holmes. "You did the right thing," he assured her. "You did what our Lord would have done." And I'd tried to imagine Jesus working at the People's Bank and calling up Golden Frinks on the telephone.

As for me, I soon came to the conclusion that integrated lunch counters would be just fine—libraries and movie theaters, too. But when it came to the schools, I had my worries. There'd been rumors that the courts would eventually force the school district to divide itself right down the center of Broad Street, with all children living on the west side assigned to Edenton Elementary and John A. Holmes High (no relation to Mr. Holmes, the minister) and those on my side of the street going to D. F. Walker. That meant

I'd be separated from my closest friends, who all lived on the west side—but even worse, I'd never get to achieve my lifelong dream of becoming a John A. Holmes High cheerleader or majorette.

Sure, D. F. Walker had its own band and cheerleaders, but it just wasn't the same. They got to march only once a year, before their annual Homecoming game. The John A. Holmes High band, with its shiny instruments and spiffy blue-and-gold uniforms, held parades practically every Friday night throughout football season. I'd always envisioned myself right there with them—twirling my baton or shaking my pom-poms and smiling at the adoring crowds.

So far, the all-white school board had resisted court orders and the NAACP's demands to integrate, and I quietly hoped they'd continue to stall—at least until I could make it through high school.

Miss Copeland's classroom. Rosemary and I are in the last two seats of the far-right row.

9. Crime and Punishment at Edenton Elementary

"As smart as he is, he sure can be lazy," I overheard Mama say to my aunt Mae one Sunday afternoon on the farm. "Sometimes I think Helen's a lot smarter."

No way! I thought. Barely ten, I was still young enough to believe just about everything my mother said, but not this. *Nobody* was smarter than my brother, Norfleet.

Sure, I got straight A's on my report card while he got an occasional B in penmanship. And I was better organized, too—always finishing my homework before supper instead of putting it off until later in the evening like he often did. Just that past fall, he'd waited until the night before it was due to even come up with an idea for his seventh-grade science project. But it didn't seem to matter, because during the hour after I went to bed, he'd gathered up his entire rock collection, labeled each specimen with its origin and type, and created a giant poster that described the difference between *igneous*, *sedimentary*, and *metamorphic*. That pulled-together-at-the-last-minute "Minerals of North Carolina" project not only earned him an A, but also a blue ribbon in the school-wide science fair.

From what I could tell, there were two reasons for my brother's so-called laziness. One was that he was so confident that he'd eventually get his work done, it didn't matter how long he procrastinated. The other was his intellectual curiosity. He had so many different interests that they often took priority over humdrum school assignments. As soon as his monthly Landmark biography arrived in the mail, he'd sit right down and read it from cover to cover, no matter how much homework awaited him. He liked current events, too—always watching the six o'clock news and documentaries on TV and reading the entire Sunday *New York Times*, even though it was sometimes three inches thick.

As for me, I preferred sitcoms over news shows, *The Bobbsey Twins* over biographies, and *Little Lulu* comics over newspapers. But even so, I had big ears and a good memory—so I'd halfway listen in as Mama and Norfleet discussed the headlines or the latest Landmark book, and then I'd go to school and drop names I'd heard like Nikita Khrushchev or J. Edgar Hoover and share facts like "The Battle of the Alamo took place in 1836." And the teachers would say to my mother, "That daughter of yours, she sure is smart!"

I suppose it was my reputation as a smart student that earned me a spot on the Student Council during the spring of 1961. As my fourth-grade classroom's representative, I not only got to attend Friday morning meetings with fifth and sixth graders, but twice a week I was excused from class a half hour before my own recess so I could monitor early recess, which was the one for children in grades one through three. An added bonus was that I got to do it with my best friend, Rosemary, daughter of our minister and the representative from another fourth-grade classroom.

With clipboard in hand and yellow "Recess Monitor" vests covering our chests, we'd meet on the front steps to begin our shift. Then, circling the schoolyard, we'd first pass the girls and boys who played hopscotch or tag in the well-kept areas closest to the building. Dressed in stylish jumpers or tucked-in oxford-cloth shirts, these were the popular children who in a year or two might become Student Council representatives like us. As our path widened, we'd find the not-quite-so-well-dressed boys and girls who played their own games of hopscotch and tag in the gravelly dirt that made up most of the schoolyard. Then, just before the bell rang to end early recess, we'd finally reach the outer perimeter, where the trailer-park and mill-village children congregated near the chain-link fence. With their hand-me-down clothing and long stringy hair, they were much more raggedy than their classmates—and older, too, as many had been "held back" a year or two. If we were looking for misbehavior, this was as likely a place as any to find it, for many of them already had reputations as troublemakers.

But Rosemary and I weren't really looking for trouble. Six weeks into the job, we hadn't turned in a single name—not because there wasn't anything to report, but because most days we were much more interested in chatting and giggling with each other than in keeping an eye out for things like gum-chewing, rock-throwing, and littering. And even if we'd come across something inappropriate, we probably wouldn't have reported it because number one, taking the time to do so would cause us to miss part of our own recess, which immediately followed; and number two, we were both scared to death of Miss Copeland, the sixth-grade teacher who served as Student Council advisor.

She stood no higher than her tallest student and was as slim as a reed, but with a mere glance from behind her tortoise-shell glasses, Miss Copeland could make the most brazen bully tremble. Her temper was legendary—you could hear her outbursts all the way down the hall—and nothing angered her more than incompetence, laziness, and what she called "poor citizenship." Her standards for her students were high, but those for the Student Council were even higher. During weekly meetings, she'd chastise anyone who was tardy or used poor grammar or violated Robert's Rules of Order—and I'd cower in the back of the room, hoping I'd never have to cross her path.

But one morning in late April, I had no choice, for I'd come across an offense that was so egregious that I knew I had to report it. While patrolling the playground alone (Rosemary was home sick with the pinkeye), I saw a third grader pick up rocks from the gravelly dirt on the outer perimeter of the schoolyard and hurl them through the chain-link fence toward the passing cars. I knew exactly who he was, for he was a known troublemaker. I also knew that if I didn't report him, somebody else would, and I might get into trouble for negligence. So I began scribbling his name on my clipboard just as the bell rang to end early recess.

Not wanting to miss too much of my own recess, I hightailed it into the school building, climbed the creaky wooden stairwell two steps at a time, and practically sprinted down the long, musty corridor toward Miss Copeland's classroom. The door was half-opened, and I gently tapped on its edge.

"So what do you have for me?" Miss Copeland barked from behind her large pine desk, key in hand, black leather purse draped over her elbow, clearly ready to retreat to the Teachers' Lounge for her own version of recess.

"I-I-I need to report an incident," I stammered.

"Well, come on out with it, child!" she demanded. "I haven't got all day."

"M-M-Michael was throwing rocks at cars."

She stared at me for a second. "Michael who?" she snapped. "Surely he has a last name."

I looked down at my clipboard to find only the word *Michael.* In my haste to make the report, I'd omitted the last name. My heart began to pound as I struggled to remember it.

"I'm waiting," said Miss Copeland, slowly lifting her glasses from the chain around her neck and placing them over her small, dark eyes. I braced myself, anticipating a scolding—but then out of the blue, a name popped into my head.

"It's Wilson!" I cried jubilantly. "His name is Michael Wilson!"

"Well, that's more like it!" Miss Copeland shouted as she motioned for me to sit in the wooden armchair next to her desk (the Student Council's version of a witness stand). "Stay here while I summon him," she said. "We need to deal with this immediately."

As I waited for her return, I stared at the large clock on the rear wall of the classroom. Nearly ten minutes of my own recess were already gone, and if she didn't hurry back, I'd miss it all. To pass the time, I walked over to the bulletin board display beneath the clock and began reading about how a bill becomes a law and the qualities of a good Student Council representative

—*responsibility, honesty,* and *integrity.* I straightened my yellow "Recess Monitor" vest.

When I eventually heard footsteps coming from down the hall, I scurried back to the chair—relieved that I'd soon be able to join my friends outside. But when Miss Copeland appeared in the classroom doorway with a frightened young boy in tow, I froze. The boy was named Michael all right, and he was one of the raggedy trailer-park children who congregated in the outer boundaries of the schoolyard. But he wasn't the Michael I'd seen throwing rocks. The name suddenly came to me. It had been Michael *Olsen*, not Michael *Wilson.*

Of course the right thing to do would have been to speak up, to admit my mistake, to apologize to the boy—and I'd like to think that's what I would have done. But before I could even find my voice, Michael Wilson confessed to the crime of throwing rocks.

What happened next is a blur. I didn't hear Miss Copeland's scathing diatribe. I didn't see her reach for the ruler. I didn't see the poor boy cringe. I was only aware of my own relief—relief that I wouldn't be reprimanded for negligence, that my reputation was intact, that I could finally go outside and enjoy the last few minutes of my own recess.

If there'd been any immediate pangs of guilt, I quickly rationalized them away. *Michael Wilson was probably throwing rocks just like the other Michael,* I told myself. *Otherwise, why would he confess?*

But guilt, I'd soon discover, can't be so easily erased. That night as I tossed and turned in bed, I couldn't stop thinking about what I'd done to poor Michael. *Maybe I should talk to Mama or Norfleet about it,* I thought—but I knew I wouldn't like what they'd have to say. Mama would surely scold me for being dishonest and unkind to someone less fortunate; and Norfleet, who at age twelve was already "Mr. Liberty and Justice for All," would insist that I march right back into Miss Copeland's classroom the next morning and exonerate Michael Wilson of any wrongdoing.

Unlike Norfleet, I wasn't born with a sense of fairness—it was something I'd have to learn. So as I closed my eyes one more time, hoping that sleep would put the day behind me, an image etched itself into the recesses of my mind—there to haunt me, there to instruct. It was of young Michael standing in the classroom doorway, his shoulders slumped, his pale blue eyes filled with resignation. "If it's my word against hers," they seemed to say, "I haven't got a chance."

Me in my Yankees uniform.

10. Home Run Heroes

By the time I entered fifth grade that fall, most of the girls in my class had crushes—not yet on boys at school, but on rock-'n-'roll idols like Elvis Presley and Ricky Nelson or TV characters like Little Joe Cartwright on *Bonanza* and Tod on *Route 66*. "Isn't he sooooo dreamy!" they'd gush at recess, and I'd pretend that I agreed.

Truth be told, I had no interest in any of them, not even Richard Chamberlain, who Rosemary flipped over after watching the first episode of *Dr. Kildare*. Sure, I thought Elvis was cute, and I would have traded old Dr. Williams for that handsome TV doctor in a heartbeat—but I couldn't imagine how anybody in her right mind could be gaga over somebody she didn't even know. At least that's what I thought until the morning of October 2, 1961.

It was almost time for Mama to drive us to school, and as usual, Norfleet was lollygagging. "Hurry up!" I yelled from the hallway. "I don't want to get marked 'tardy' because of you!" Then

I barged into his room and found him lying on the floor, still in pajamas, reading the *Raleigh News & Observer* sports page.

"I can't believe you're not even dressed!" I shouted. "We need to be out the door in five minutes."

"He did it," Norfleet said calmly, completely oblivious to my frazzled state.

"Who did what?" I snapped.

He pointed to the newspaper's black-and-white photograph of Roger Maris swinging at his sixty-first home run, the most anybody had ever hit in a single season. "Maris just broke Babe Ruth's record."

I squatted down to look, but my attention was immediately drawn to another picture at the bottom of the page, a close-up of Maris peering from beneath his New York Yankees cap, grinning at the camera. Sure, I'd seen him on TV many a time, for I regularly watched the *Game of the Week* with Granddaddy, but I'd never really looked at his face. There was a sweetness about it—a kindness to his smile, a shyness in his pale eyes. It suddenly dawned on me that he was much more handsome than Frankie Avalon or Little Joe Cartwright or even Dr. Kildare. *He's the one!* I said to myself. And just like that, I fell in love.

In retrospect, it's not surprising that my first crush would be on a baseball star. I'd always liked the sport—playing catch with Norfleet in the backyard, enjoying the occasional Sunday afternoon pickup game on the farm, and of course watching the *Game of the Week* on television. But once I made Roger Maris my idol, baseball was no longer just a pastime. It became my passion.I followed the 1961 World Series closely, watching as much as I could on TV. I memorized box scores from the newspaper. I pasted pictures and articles about Maris on my bedroom door. Granddaddy, who'd always liked baseball, was thrilled with my new interest. Although he didn't believe in spending money on presents, he ordered me my very own New York Yankees uniform from the Sears Roebuck catalog.

When I marched into the Nu-Curl Beauty Salon that fall and asked for a haircut just like Roger Maris's, Mama began to worry—it was enough to have a daughter who dressed like a baseball star, but this was going a bit too far for her. "You don't need to fret about Little Helen," I overheard my aunt Mae say to her. "She's just going through a phase."

And Mae was right. By the time school let out for the summer, my hair had grown out and my obsession with Roger Maris had subsided—but not my love of baseball. I still followed the Yankees closely. And each morning after Mama left for work, Norfleet and I would go outside to throw and bat, always keeping a fishing net nearby in case one of us hit the ball into the bay.

After an hour or so of practice, we'd head up to Mitchener's, where Edenton's old-boy network huddled each morning over coffee or Cokes to discuss politics and sports, leaving their offices or stores in the care of their female assistants. Mama's boss, Mr. White, would be among them. When he'd see me heading toward the counter for a Coke, usually dressed in my Yankees uniform, he'd always ask me a question like "Who do you think will pitch against the Red Sox next Saturday, Little Helen?" And I'd always have an answer like "Whitey Ford has the best record against Yastrzemski—they'd be fools not to use him." Then, as the men slapped their thighs and snickered, I'd wonder what they found to be so funny.

By late July, I'd gotten so good at throwing, catching, and batting that Norfleet invited me to go with him to the vacant lot behind the Catholic church, where he and the other boys who'd outgrown Little League gathered for pickup games. "We never have enough players," he told me.

So later that afternoon, the two of us hopped onto our bikes, me in my pinstriped Yankees uniform, both of us with a glove in one hand, and headed up Broad Street toward St. Ann's. As we parked our bicycles on the sidewalk next to the makeshift field, the five or six boys who'd already arrived stared at me with a look that seemed to ask, "What's *she* doing here?"

Norfleet assured them I was a good player, but the two oldest boys, the self-appointed captains, looked unconvinced. They formed a huddle—probably to decide which was worse, allowing a girl to join them or not having enough players for a good game of ball. "Okay," one of them finally said. "We'll give her a try, but she'll have to play in the outfield, and she's gonna bat last."

I was a bit nervous at first and dropped an easy pop-up, but by the end of the afternoon, I'd gotten on base every single time at bat and even caught a line drive. "We'll see her tomorrow!" one of the boys shouted to Norfleet as the two of us hopped onto our bikes to return home.

By the end of the week, I'd become a regular at those afternoon games. (They always needed extras.) Then one day in early August, just as the captains had finished choosing sides, a tall, dark-skinned boy appeared on the sidewalk nearby. Neatly dressed in khaki pants and a blue button-down shirt, he looked to be just a little older than me, maybe twelve or thirteen, and he was holding a baseball glove.

"Do you need another player?" he asked, enunciating each word like a radio announcer.

The answer was obvious, for there were only six players on my team and five on the other—but we all turned toward the two captains. What were they to do? They'd just allowed a girl onto their turf, and now they were being asked to integrate it? They formed a huddle. Then after a bit of discussion, the captain with the least number of players turned toward the boy and said, using a tone that wasn't particularly friendly, "You can be on my team, but you'll have to bat last and play in the outfield."

"That's okay with me," the boy replied in a deep, almost baritone voice. "And by the way, my name is James."

My team was up first, and since I was last in the batting order, I took a seat on the scraggly grass behind the garbage-can lid that served as home plate. The leadoff batter popped up to the pitcher; the second one struck out. Then Norfleet, who batted third, hit a hard line drive toward right field, clearly a base hit—until James snagged it on first bounce and hurled it to the first baseman for an easy out.

"Nice catch," Norfleet said as our team took the field.

I positioned myself in the same spot where James had just played and watched as the first two batters grounded out to the shortstop/third baseman. The next three hit singles into left field. When James approached the plate, the bases were loaded.

The first pitch was low and inside, practically grazing his knee. "That's a strike!" shouted Elroy Jones, acting as both catcher and umpire. The next one was high and wide, but James swung at it anyway and missed. The third came fast and hard, much closer to the strike zone, and before I knew it, the ball ripped off of the bat and was heading toward me in right field. I lifted my glove, but it soared high above me. When it finally landed in the hedge between the field and the property next door, James had already rounded the bases—and I had to be reminded that it was my job to sneak into the neighbor's backyard to retrieve it.

James batted three more times that afternoon, hitting home runs every time. When the game was finally called at 12–2, the captain of the winning team walked over to him and said in a voice that the rest of us could barely hear, "See you tomorrow."

That night at dinner, when Norfleet and I told Mama about the boy who played ball like Willie Mays and spoke like a radio announcer, she placed her index finger on her temple, which was what she did when trying to figure out who someone was. (Being a teller at the People's Bank, she knew most of Edenton's citizens, black *and* white; and if she didn't know them personally, she often knew where they came from family-wise.) "I'll bet that's Erma Sander's grandboy," she said after a while. "He must be visiting from New Jersey."

"Well, that explains why he doesn't talk like the folks around here," I said.

"And that explains why he's playing baseball with the white kids," said Mama. "Things are a lot different up north."

For the remainder of the summer, James showed up at the vacant lot almost every afternoon. Although I rarely spoke to him (or to any of the other boys, for that matter), I couldn't keep my eyes off him. His athleticism was amazing to watch, but he also had a confident, easygoing manner that was different from that of most boys his age. Whenever he looked my way, I'd quickly turn away. Was it a crush? I'm not really sure. But even if it was, I wouldn't have admitted it—for there was an unspoken rule, at least in Edenton, North Carolina, that eleven-year-old white girls don't develop crushes on boys like James.

If I was in the outfield when James came up to bat, I'd back up as far as I could in hopes of preventing a homer (which I rarely did). But one afternoon toward late August, as I positioned myself at the far end of the field next to the neighbor's hedge, he hit a hard, high-bouncing grounder that somehow made its way to the inside of my outstretched glove. "Throw it here!" shouted Bobby on second, and I managed to hurl it to him just in time to hold James at first.

Next up was Elroy Jones, a notoriously weak hitter, so I moved in closer to the infield. Then as the pitcher began his windup, James took off for a steal and slid hard into the flattened cardboard box that served as second base—seconds before being tagged.

"You're out!" yelled Bobby.

"No, I'm not," replied James.

"I said you're out!" Bobby repeated, and when it became clear to him that James wasn't going anywhere, Bobby moved in closer. "If *I* say you're out, you're out," he growled, "because you're nothin' but a lyin', cheatin' nigger!"

With that, boys from both teams gathered around—and I knew I should speak up because from my vantage point only a few yards away, James was clearly safe. I took a deep breath, hoping I could muster the courage to contradict a boy who was three years older than me. But I didn't have to.

"I was safe," James said in his calm, deep voice, "and if you can't trust me to tell the truth, I refuse to ever play here again."

As a silence fell over the field, the other boys stared at Bobby with a look that seemed to say, "C'mon, buddy, we need him. Just admit you're wrong."

Bobby slowly backed away, and after a few tense moments, he mumbled, "All right, all right—I'll let you have it this time."

For the remaining days of the summer, the boys treated James differently. They shared jokes with him, sat next to him while waiting to bat, even patted him on the back when he crossed home plate. They practically treated him like he was one of them, except when choosing sides. Although James was clearly the best player on the field, he was always picked last, right after me—as though following a rule that white boys had to be chosen first (no matter how badly they played), white girls next (even though I was much better than many of the boys), and coloreds always last.

Funny thing is that neither James nor I ever complained about it. I guess we were just happy to be playing baseball.

Mama at home after work.

11. Cocktail Hour

I learned at an early age that there's a difference between happy drinking and lonely drinking. Happy drinking was what Mama did each weekend with her in-laws, who, unlike the Baptist side of the family, saw no problem with alcohol in moderation. On Fridays after work, her face would practically glow as she'd discuss politics and sip bourbon with Mag. Then on Saturday nights at Madam's house, cocktail hour would put her in such a good mood that she'd often sing along as Lina played show tunes on the piano after dinner and still be humming the melodies during the drive home later that evening.

Occasionally there'd be a weekday afternoon when an old friend would call to say, "Please stop by for a drink; you can bring the children." And as Norfleet and I sipped Cokes and ate peanuts in front of an out-of-the way TV, we'd hear our mother's throaty laugh above the din of adult conversation.

But those kinds of last-minute, weekday invitations were few and far between. ("People forget about you when you're not part of a couple," Mama once said.) Most days after work, it was just her alone—pouring a jigger of bourbon over a glass full of ice cubes, adding a splash of water, and then perching herself on the green upholstered chair that faced the window overlooking the bay. "I just need some time to unwind," she'd say while lighting up a Salem with her chrome Zippo lighter. And there she'd sit, sipping and puffing, sipping and puffing, until it was time for the six o'clock news.

One drink was usually all she needed to revive herself after a long day at work. But sometimes one wasn't enough, and there'd be another, and perhaps even a third—and Norfleet and I would brace ourselves for what might follow.

It was usually something trivial that would set her off—like not being able to find her scissors while hemming a skirt or mending a pair of trousers. "Has anybody seen my scissors?" she'd begin. And if the question went unanswered, she'd say a bit louder, "I can't ever find anything around this house!" followed by the accusation, "You children never put things back where they belong!" And then she'd rant and rave about how ungrateful we were and how she slaved away all day at the bank to be able to put food on our table, and that if we'd lived through the Great Depression as she had, we'd respect her property and appreciate the value of a dollar. With each verbal blow, Norfleet and I would hunker down, never talking back, just waiting for the storm to pass—and it always did, almost as quickly as it came, and then she'd hug us and tell us she loved us and that we meant the world to her.

One afternoon when Norfleet was away at a Boy Scout gathering, Mama arrived home from work so tired and in such a bad mood, she didn't even say hello before fixing herself a drink. "People can be such idiots," she muttered as she walked right past me, glass of bourbon in hand, toward the chair that overlooked the bay. She was angry because she'd stayed at work an extra half hour to balance her cash drawer, only to discover that a customer had carelessly written the wrong amount on a deposit slip.

Leaving her alone to sip and stew, I retreated to my room to do my homework—but when it got to be seven o'clock, our usual dinner hour, I returned to the living room. "I suppose you're getting hungry," she said when she saw me. She slowly extinguished her cigarette, rose from the green chair, and carried the empty glass into the kitchen.

"We had potpies for dinner last night," I reminded her as she pulled two Morton chicken potpies from the freezer portion of the refrigerator.

"Well, excuse *me*, Miss Priss!" she snapped, slamming the refrigerator door and walking over to the oven to set it at 350 degrees. "I don't exactly have a lot of time on my hands to fix home-cooked meals!" And with that, she launched into her usual tirade about slaving away at the bank all day to put food on the table and surviving the Great Depression, and how I didn't appreciate the value of a dollar.

I braced myself, waiting for the storm to pass. But as she approached the end, the part where she was supposed to tell me she loved me and that I meant the world to her, she blurted out, "Sometimes I wish I were dead!"

I don't know if she heard my gasp or just realized the horror of her words—but as my tears began to flow, she reached out to embrace me.

"Please don't die, Mama!" I sobbed, melting into her arms.

"Don't worry, Sweetie," she replied, her voice now calm and kind, "I'm not going anywhere—not if I can help it."

Of course I wanted to believe her, but that night at bedtime, I resurrected a prayer I hadn't said in years: *Please, dear God, don't let Mama get cancer and die like Daddy.*

12. The Facts of Life

I was only looking for a pencil—one to replace the yellow number-2 I'd broken while doing my sixth-grade arithmetic homework. The chest next to Mama's bed was as likely a place as any to find one because most nights she worked on the Sunday *New York Times* crossword before bedtime, penciling in the words one by one, often taking an entire week to complete the grid. As expected, there was a folded, half-completed puzzle inside the top drawer, along with several well-sharpened pencils held together with a pink rubber band. But right there next to them were a few items I didn't expect to find—a small gold satchel wrapped in plastic and labeled *Teenage by Modess: 2 Napkins Inside*, a junior-sized sanitary belt, and two thin booklets entitled *Growing Up and Liking It* and *How Shall I Tell My Daughter?*

It took only a half second for me to realize they were meant for me, for I was almost twelve, and according to Kay Crosby, who was two years older than me, twelve or thirteen was the age when most girls started having periods. She'd told me all about it during vacation at Nags Head the previous summer; and although I wasn't very interested in the subject at the time, I was now intrigued. I took a seat on the edge of Mama's bed and began flipping through the pages of *Growing Up and Liking It.*

There were photographs of pretty teenage girls primping, chatting on the phone, and going on dates with boys. There were diagrams of uteruses and fallopian tubes. When I got to a section called "What happens when you grow up?" I stopped my flipping and began reading about the bodily changes that precede menstruation:

> *Her straight-up-and-down figure begins to develop graceful curves … her breasts begin to fill out and she discovers the start of a real waistline and hips. She also develops a soft growth of hair under her arms and on the lower abdomen (called the pubic area).*

I looked down at my still-boyish figure, feeling a combination of distress and relief. The distress was because I was perfectly happy with the way I was, straight-up-and-down figure and all, and I couldn't imagine myself with breasts, pubic hair, and graceful curves. The relief was that my undeveloped body was nowhere near ready for things like sanitary belts or Modess pads. I carefully placed the booklet back into the drawer, grabbed a pencil, and went back to my room to finish my homework before Mama got home from work.

I tried to forget about my discovery, but of course I couldn't. So the next day at school I told Rosemary, who of course wanted to see *Growing Up and Liking It* for herself. So that very afternoon, the two of us sneaked back into Mama's room, removed the booklet from the drawer, and took turns reading. We read about teenage moodiness, we got tips on personal hygiene, and we learned about the preparation of the uterus for a baby. But we could find absolutely nothing on the subject that interested us the most—how a baby might get there. There was nothing that verified what Norfleet had told me a few weeks before during a Saturday morning game of Crazy Eights.

"You're a liar!" I'd shouted as I tossed the deck of cards in his face. Mama had taught me that private parts should remain private, and I couldn't imagine anybody in their right mind doing what he'd described. But then as he calmly picked up the cards from the living room floor, he explained that his information was from a very reliable source—from Donny Douglas, who was the youngest cousin of Joe Harper, who was best friends with Johnny Burns, who'd gotten Betty Sue Smith pregnant. I'd remembered the adult gossip—what a shame, they'd said, having to get married so young and her having to drop out of high school. So later that day over Cokes at Mitchener's, I told Rosemary what Norfleet had told me, and she'd almost fallen off the soda fountain stool. It was hard enough for me to imagine Mama doing it twice to have my brother and me, but for her, the oldest of our minister's nine children, it was more than four times as shocking.

When it was clear that *Growing Up and Liking It* didn't contain the information we were seeking, Rosemary and I flipped through *How Shall I Tell My Daughter?* But there was nothing there either—just the same information about bodily changes and sanitary products, along with tips to mothers on when to bring up the subject of menstruation. "When your daughter shows signs of maturing physically," the booklet suggested, "or when her friends begin to menstruate."

Before I knew it, the school year ended and it was time for our annual two-week vacation at Nags Head. Mag wouldn't be arriving until the second week, so Kay Crosby and her mother were invited to join us for a few days—a tradition that began the year before, after the death of Kay's father. Mama was glad to have a fellow widow to sip cocktails with on the wraparound porches that lined the Atlantic shoreline. And since Norfleet now spent most of his time with the boys from neighboring cottages, I was glad to have a girl to play with, even though she was two years older.

The previous summer when Kay told me about periods, our age gap had hardly been noticeable. We both enjoyed dressing our Barbie dolls, playing Wiffle Ball in the sand, and discussing Nancy Drew. But this year things were different. Now almost fourteen and a good six inches taller than me, Kay had the figure of a full-grown woman, was more interested in movie stars than fictional detectives, and wouldn't be caught dead playing dolls or Wiffle Ball with a twelve-year-old. If not for the fact that there were no other teenage girls nearby, she probably would have ignored me.

Determined to get a good tan, Kay insisted that we spend much of the day on the beach in front of Mag's cottage. Stretched out on our towels, we'd flip through *Seventeen* and *Photoplay* magazines, discuss movie star gossip, and watch fellow beachgoers walk past us at the water's edge—mainly mothers with children, but there'd be the occasional dad, who'd subtly turn our way to get a good look at Kay in her form-fitting white eyelet swimsuit.

One morning as we basked in the hot July sun, a skinny woman with a huge belly waddled past us to retrieve a little boy who had dashed into the surf. We giggled at her awkwardness. Then Kay turned toward me and asked with a mischievous grin, "You *do* know how women get pregnant, don't you?"

"Of course I do!" I responded. "It's disgusting!"

Kay began rubbing baby oil and iodine onto her already tan legs. "No, it isn't," she said softly. "Making love is a beautiful thing." She slowly tossed her thick, brown hair behind her back. "And it all begins with holding hands."

I gasped. Just that past spring I'd held hands with George Wheeler at the sixth-grade square dance, and although his sweaty palms had made me uncomfortable, I'd had no idea that hand-holding led to babies. I moved my beach towel closer, eager to hear more.

Kay was now rubbing the reddish-brown concoction onto her shoulders, being careful not to stain her white eyelet straps. "Holding hands is just first base," she explained, and then she went on to describe the entire lovemaking process in terms of baseball. She personally had only gone as far as second base—with Robbie Atkins at the Methodist Youth Fellowship hayride. And although it was very tempting to go all the way to home plate, she was going to save that for marriage because number one, she had a reputation to protect, and number two, she didn't want to end up like poor Betty Sue Smith, who'd had to step down from the cheerleading squad and drop out of high school to have a baby.

Kay's explanation was much more detailed than my brother's had been, and by the time she finished talking, my head was spinning. "I'm gonna take a dip," I said, hoping the cold water would help.

When I returned to my towel ten minutes later, I found Kay lying facedown with her swimsuit top completely unstrapped so she wouldn't get a tan line. Sopping wet and still in a bit of a tizzy, I tugged at the straps of my yellow striped tank suit (Girls

Department, size 12). Then I reached into my beach bag, removed Norfleet's latest issue of *Sports Illustrated*, and began reading about how Roger Maris was helping to keep the Yankees in first place while Mickey Mantle recovered from an injury. The article immediately calmed me—and even though I was no longer gaga over the Yankee slugger, I was glad to know he was doing well. At least for now, I'd stick to *real* baseball.

When I entered John A. Holmes High as a seventh grader that fall, I discovered that many of the girls in my class had started menstruating over the summer and many more were wearing bras. I still showed no signs of development, but now that I was at school with teenagers rather than elementary school children, I was beginning to think of myself differently. I imagined being all shapely like Kay Crosby, tossing my hair behind my back and being whistled at by boys—which, of course, was pure fantasy because my chest was still flat as a pancake, my hair was too short to toss, and no boys were inspired to whistle at me. Clearly I was a late bloomer, but at least I was no longer frightened by the prospect of womanhood.

"We need to talk," Mama said one September afternoon as I headed to my room to finish my homework. She was seated on the living room sofa, a glass of bourbon in one hand—and there on the coffee table next to her was *Growing Up and Liking It*. She motioned for me to sit, and as she slowly lit up a Salem, I knew the time had finally arrived for her to tell me about the facts of life.

As I joined her on the sofa, she took a deep, slow drag from her cigarette. "You're growing up, Sweetie," she began.

"Yes, ma'am," I replied.

"And soon you'll be having periods like other girls."

"Yes, ma'am," I replied again.

"When a girl is about thirteen years old, her body begins to prepare for the future time when she can be a mother. . . ." With her eyes on her cocktail rather than on me, she spoke in a monotone, and it sounded to me as though she'd memorized the verbiage from *How Shall I Tell My Daughter*.

She paused for moment, and I wasn't sure whether she was waiting for me to respond or had simply forgotten the next line. In either case, she seemed so ill-at-ease that I decided to help her out.

"I already know that stuff," I said.

She looked surprised. "How do you know?"

I wasn't about to tell her about sneaking into her bedside drawer and finding the Modess starter kit, so I said, "Kay Crosby told me. She told me all about it at Nags Head."

Mama took a sip of bourbon and then extinguished her cigarette. If she'd planned to follow the script laid out in *How Shall I Tell My Daughter?* I certainly hadn't helped matters.

"She told me about making love, too," I said, hoping to end the conversation and put her out of her misery.

Mama smiled for a moment, as though amused by my word choice. Then she got all serious again. "Well, it sounds like Kay Crosby has beaten me to the punch," she said, and I wasn't sure if I was hearing relief or disappointment in her voice.

"I love you, Mama," I blurted out, for lack of anything better to say. Then after she said it back, I rose from the sofa, assuming our talk was over.

"Wait a minute!" she shouted as I made my way to the doorway. "Here's something I've been meaning to give you." She was holding up the copy of *Growing Up and Liking It.*

"Oh, thank you!" I said as I flipped through its pages. Not wanting to spoil my mother's good intentions, I pretended I was reading it for the very first time.

13. The Funeral

EDENTON, NC – Services for Miss Margaret Hines Pruden, who died suddenly Sunday evening, will be held at 11 a.m., Tuesday, at St. Paul's Episcopal Church, Edenton, with the Reverend George B. Holmes officiating. A native of Edenton, Miss Pruden, 80, was the daughter of the late Mary Norfleet Pruden and the late William Dossey Pruden, a prominent Edenton attorney who served as an officer in the Confederate army and was mayor of Edenton and president of the North Carolina Bar Association. Miss Pruden is survived by a niece, Mrs. George K. Mack of Edenton; a nephew, Mr. Jack McMullen Pruden of Chapel Hill; and five grand nieces and nephews, including Helen Goodwin Pruden and James Norfleet Pruden III of Edenton, children of Miss Pruden's late nephew, James Norfleet Pruden, Jr. of Edenton. (Death notice published in local papers, December 10, 1963.)

Mag passed away on the night of my thirteenth birthday, and although Dr. Williams said it was a stroke, I believed otherwise. From what I could tell, she'd begun dying two weeks earlier—not from a clotted blood vessel, but from grief over the president's assassination.

From the moment he took office, President Kennedy also captured a piece of my great-aunt's heart. Throughout our Friday night dinners, she'd rave about his youthful vigor, his elegant style, and those stirring speeches, many of which she could quote by heart. "Ask not what your country can do for you," she'd say with tears of emotion welling in her eyes, "ask what you can do for your country."

"If I didn't know any better, Miss Margaret, I'd say you had a crush on the president," Mama once teased after hearing about that "winning Kennedy smile" for the umpteenth time.

"Don't be ridiculous!" replied my spinster great-aunt, but I could tell from her reddening face that Mama was on to something.

Whenever President Kennedy spoke on TV, Mag held onto every word. Whatever he did, she always approved. When he called for a nationwide fallout shelter program, she ordered a set of blueprints from the Civil Defense Department and then talked for weeks about erecting a shelter in her basement. When he defied Governor Wallace and sent federal troops to integrate the University of Alabama, she defended the decision.

"It was the right thing to do," she said at dinner one Friday, not long after the president spoke about it on TV. "No one should be denied the right to a decent education."

Mama, Norfleet, and I looked at her with astonishment. We knew she supported education for everyone. (She gave regularly to the United Negro College Fund.) But we also knew she favored *separate* education. "Haven't you always been against integrated schools?" asked Norfleet, who at age fifteen had a knack for questioning adults without sounding rude or impertinent.

"The president had to uphold the law," Mag replied. And I wondered if this was the same great-aunt who only a few weeks earlier had reprimanded me for referring to the St. Paul's janitor as "Mr. Austin," the term the Holmes children used at the rectory. "His name is *Vance*," she'd told me in no uncertain terms. "Coloreds should be addressed only by their first names." And even though I'd spent my entire life referring to maids and yardmen as Vanzula, Lucy, or Red without even considering the fact that they had surnames, I'd said, "That makes no sense," to which Mag replied, "That's just the way it is." Maybe Mag saw law and custom as two completely different things.

The news of the assassination stunned us all, but it hit Mag especially hard. When we arrived for dinner on that awful Friday in November, she was so distraught she could hardly speak. So we spent the entire evening in the TV room, switching back and forth between Walter Cronkite and Chet Huntley as we ate our dinner from trays. When Lucy lingered in the doorway after serving us, Mag invited her to bring in her own tray and watch TV with us. This was something neither she nor Lucy would normally do, but we were all so united by our grief that night, nobody seemed to care about custom.

On December 8, the day I turned thirteen, Mag was still in such a state of despair, she didn't attend services at St. Paul's. So we stopped by to check on her before heading to the farm for Sunday lunch. When she met us at the door, her blue-gray hair uncombed, her green wool dress hanging unbelted from her thinner-than-ever frame, she looked as though she'd just rolled out of bed even though it was already half past noon. "Happy birthday, Little Helen," she said with forced cheerfulness. "I didn't have it in me to go shopping this year, so you'll have to buy your own present."

"This is perfect!" I beamed as I looked down at the ten-dollar check she'd handed me—glad that for once I wasn't getting a book I'd never read, a sweater I'd never wear, or toiletries I'd never use. I was already imagining myself in that cute, lace-collared cardigan I'd just seen in the Betty Shoppe window.

We stayed for only a few minutes, just long enough to hear about the latest developments in the assassination investigation. Then as we prepared to leave, I saw Mag hand my brother a folded piece of paper.

"She gave *you* money on *my* birthday?" I shouted when we got into the car and I learned it was a check. While I felt more at home with Mama's side of the family, Norfleet, with his braininess and "III" attached to his name, was the golden boy of the Pruden side—something that normally didn't bother me, except on a day when *I* was supposed to be the special one.

Norfleet tried to explain that the check was to cover his travel expenses to the State Science Fair. "Didn't she just pay for you to attend the glee club concert in Greenville?" he asked in an attempt at justification.

"But today is *my* birthday!" I screamed. "Couldn't she at least wait a day?" I ranted all the way to the farm. "You've always been her favorite," I fumed. "She's so unfair!"

"Now, now, Helen," said Mama from the driver's seat.

"I hate her!" I hissed.

It can be confusing when a loved one dies while you're still angry at her. If I'd heard the news only one day before, I would have wept and talked about how much she meant to me. But when we got the early Monday phone call, I didn't gasp or moan or even shed a tear. Then, as Mama wondered aloud about plans for the burial, I wondered to myself, "Will I still be able to cash the check?"

It was my first funeral, and I had nothing black to wear. Mama said my navy wool skirt and jacket would be fine, but when the three of us arrived at the St. Paul's churchyard and I saw only shades of black and gray, I wondered if I was dressed appropriately.

After entering the old brick church, we took our regular seats in the Pruden family pew, where my ancestors had worshipped for nearly two centuries and where for as long as I could remember, I'd sat next to Mag during Sunday morning services. But I wasn't thinking about either of those facts—or about the coffin, draped in white, at the base of the altar. My mind instead was on the tiny tear in the knee of my navy-blue leggings, and I hoped it wouldn't become larger.

"'I am the resurrection and the life,' saith the Lord," began Mr. Holmes after the processional. Dressed in a white alb with a white embroidered stole hanging from his shoulders and wearing a somber expression on his face, he seemed so different from the normally jovial minister who often told jokes during Sunday morning sermons.

"Glory be to thee, O Lord," the congregation responded, and I scanned the surrounding pews to see if anyone else was dressed in navy. The readings from the Gospel followed, then the eulogy, and when the choir began singing "Jesu, Joy of Man's Desiring," my eyes finally rested on the casket.

Although draped in white instead of the American flag, it made me think of the casket where President Kennedy was laid in state a little over two weeks before. The television images were still so fresh in my mind—the thousands of mourners filing past it in the Capitol Rotunda, the military caisson carrying it toward Arlington Cemetery, and little John-John, barely three, bravely saluting as it passed. "I will lift up mine eyes unto the hills, from whence cometh my strength," Mr. Holmes said loudly, jarring me back to the here and now.

We all stood to sing "O God Our Help in Ages Past," and as the pallbearers lifted Mag's casket and carried it down the stone-paved aisle, Mama, Norfleet, and I followed close behind, slowly making our way through the open doors and into the leafless December churchyard. With hundreds of moss-covered tombstones dating back as far as the early 1700s, it had just about reached its capacity, which was why most parishioners (including Daddy) were now buried at Beaver Hill, the whites-only cemetery located just outside of town. But my great-grandfather had planned ahead and ensured that his two spinster daughters, Mag and her sister Mary, who died before I was born, would be laid to rest beside him. Mag's plot was freshly dug, and as the three of us took our places on its edge, I buttoned up my navy jacket to protect myself from the cold, damp wind.

"Into thy hands, O Lord, we commend they servant," continued Mr. Holmes. As I tried to listen to his words, I imagined that Mama, Norfleet, and I were Jackie, John-John, and Caroline—Jackie so dignified and beautiful in her black lace mantilla, her children there on each side of her. I thought about how Caroline had been just about the same age as I was when *my* father died, and I wondered if she missed him. Then I thought about the *Life* magazine photographs of the assassination and Jackie's splattered Chanel suit—red on pink, just like Daddy's blood on the pink linoleum bathroom floor.

And that's when the crying began—silently at first, and I gently daubed my eyes with the folded Kleenex I'd kept inside my coat pocket. But the tears kept coming, and before I knew it, I was chortling and heaving so audibly that Mama put her arm around my shoulder to calm me and Norfleet handed me his own folded tissue. Mr. Holmes had to raise his voice to be heard above my racket, and it wasn't until the casket was lowered into the earth that my crying finally stopped.

The festive atmosphere in my great-aunt's living room was not how I'd envisioned a funeral reception. It had been planned by my aunt Nancy and uncle Jack (Daddy's younger brother), who'd arrived from Chapel Hill the day before, and I was suddenly angry at them for throwing what looked like a party without Mag there to enjoy it. Flowers were everywhere, and the antique tongue-and-groove desk, where Mag always read her mail in the late afternoon, had been converted into a bar complete with glassware, bottles of bourbon, and a silver bucket of ice.

Self-conscious about my tear-stained face, I tried to weave my way past the conversational clusters toward the empty chair in the corner of the room. Along the way, people stopped me to say, "She's in a better place," or "It's all for the best," or "At least she didn't suffer," and I'd do my best to smile and nod.

When I finally reached my destination, I saw Lucy enter the room, all dressed up in her maid's uniform and carrying a tray of sandwiches. Her lips were pursed, as though she, too, was put off by the reveling, but when she saw me, she smiled and headed my way. "Are you all right, child?" she asked. "I've never heard so much sobbin' in all my born days!"

"You were at the funeral?" I asked with surprise, for I surely would have noticed her among St. Paul's all-white congregation.

"Me and Red was just there in the churchyard for the burial," she said, referring to Red the gardener. "We both thought the world of Miss Margaret and wanted to see her put to rest."

As I looked into her sad, dark eyes, it suddenly occurred to me that with my great-aunt's passing, she'd no longer have a job. "She thought the world of you, too," I said, wishing Lucy could stand there next to me throughout the reception. But she had sandwiches to serve, and as she left my side to carry out her duties, Mr. Holmes headed my way, no longer wearing the white funeral alb, but rather his black clerical suit with its white collar.

"They that sow tears shall reap joy," he said, quoting from the book of Psalms. "It's healthy to cry over a loved one's death." And although I knew he was simply offering consolation, I wanted to shout, "I wasn't crying about Mag—I was crying about the president!" But I wasn't really sure if that was the case.

There were so many unexpected feelings churning inside me—anger, a little bit of guilt, and a sadness so deep I couldn't put a finger on it. The only thing I knew for sure was that I was embarrassed about falling apart in the churchyard. Then as Mr. Holmes continued to quote from Psalms and assured me that Mag was now at peace, I vowed to myself that I'd never again cry at a funeral. Not ever.

14. The Two Sisters

Mawmaw's funeral was nothing like Mag's. Held a year and a half later in the middle of August, it was a simple graveside service at Beaver Hill Cemetery. Mainly family was there, but also the Yeopim Baptist choir, made up of my grandmother's country friends, many of them old and decrepit. Their *a cappella* rendition of "In the Sweet By and By" was nasal and off-key, causing the cousins to giggle and making it easy for me not to cry.

Of course I was sad about Mawmaw's passing, but it had come as no surprise. She'd been bedridden and on the edge of death since her first heart attack in June. Although Mama had wanted to keep her in the hospital, my aunt Mae insisted that she be brought to *her* house, where she'd converted the den into a sickroom. "Well, suit yourself," Mama said after days of arguing, which was surprising to me because Mama usually came out ahead in those sisterly spats.

For as long as I could remember, the two of them were always fighting over something—such as whether to serve a lime Jell-O mold or tomato aspic at Mawmaw and Granddaddy's fifty-fifth anniversary dinner (Mama won—we had aspic) or about my aunt's new, wood-laminate kitchen table, which Mama said looked cheap, causing Mae to cry. Then there was the time when Mae accused Mama of quoting the *New York Times* as if it were the Holy Bible, and Mama quickly retorted, "Well, at least I read something besides *Good Housekeeping*."

"If you and Mae love each other, why do you fight so much?" I once asked. "We don't fight; we bicker," Mama replied. "That's what sisters do."

Mama was six years older and two inches taller, but it was obvious the two were sisters. Blessed with Coke-bottle figures, they carried themselves with the same erect posture as my grandmother. They both had thick, curly hair that became sophisticated shades of "salt and pepper" by the time they'd reached age forty; green-gray eyes, which Granddaddy called "cat's eyes"; and jaws that matched the squareness of their hairlines. Not exactly pretty, they were what most people would call "fine-looking women."

But as similar as they were in appearance, their temperaments couldn't have been more different. Norfleet and I sometimes joked that if they were typecast to be in *Gone with the Wind*, which was shown every few years at the Taylor Theater, Mama would have been the hands-down choice for Scarlett, and Mae the perfect Melanie. Like Scarlett, Mama was feisty, short-tempered, and a bit vain about her appearance. She could be charming and witty (also a bit sarcastic), and she had a steely determination that made her believe she could handle anything.

Mae, on the other hand, was all about sweetness and goodness. She didn't drink or smoke, never said *goddamnit,* and rarely raised her voice, even to her children. She brought pies to shut-ins, taught Vacation Bible School at Edenton Baptist, and could be counted on by her neighbors to gather mail and feed their pets while they were away.

After finishing high school, the two had taken different paths—Mama living on her own before marrying Daddy, and Mae immediately marrying her high school sweetheart, the teetotaling son of a Baptist minister, who after serving in the navy worked his way up from clerk to part owner of the town's menswear and shoe store. While Mama enjoyed cocktail parties and movies, Mae preferred Wednesday night prayer meetings. While Mama belonged to a bridge group and was active in the Edenton Women's Club, Mae limited her social affiliations to family and church. While Mama was friendly with many of the town's black citizens and had entrusted the care of her house and children to maids, Mae believed that "birds of a feather should flock together" and would never even consider allowing a person of color onto her property. Until Mawmaw's death, the two sisters didn't seem to have much in common. But now they were united by a mutual cause—the care and feeding of my grandfather.

"You can't live out there by yourself," they told him, but he was intent on returning home after the funeral. To Granddaddy's way of thinking, the farm was where he'd spent most of his life, and by golly, it was where he was going to die. If he could survive droughts, hurricanes, and the Great Depression, he could certainly handle living alone.

He'd flatly refused Mae's offer to stay in the converted den, where he'd slept on the couch the past month next to Mawmaw's rented hospital bed. And he wouldn't even consider Mama's idea to purchase a motor home and park it in our driveway. "There's no way I'm gonna live inside a metal box!" he said. "My best memories of Jennie are out on the farm, and that's where I intend to be."

So he headed out Mae's driveway in his little red Falcon, which had been the cheapest car on the lot when he'd finally traded in his old, run-down Plymouth. "Well, at least he can enjoy the plumbing," Mama said sarcastically while waving goodbye. "I'm sure he'll try to live long enough to get his money's worth." For decades, Mawmaw had begged in vain for an indoor toilet. "Too expensive," my grandfather had told her; "the outhouse works just fine." "But you can't take it with you, Papa!" the aunts and uncles nagged, referring to his untouched savings account and his regular income from the leasing of his fields. So to shut them all up, he'd finally converted a downstairs closet into a bathroom—only a year or two before Mawmaw died.

When the Falcon was no longer in sight, the three of us walked back into Mae's small, brick house, where my cousin Ann, six years older than me, was already cleaning up from the small family gathering that had followed the funeral. "We have no control over where he sleeps," Mama said as she and Mae gathered the remaining paper cups and plates from the living room and carried them into the kitchen, "but we can at least make sure he eats."

"You're right," Mae agreed. And before I knew it, the two of them were sitting down at the kitchen table (the one Mama had called cheap) and figuring out their strategy.

The plan was simple. Mae would do the grocery shopping

once a week—mainly cans of soup and tuna, because Granddaddy had never learned to cook for himself. Mama, in turn, would persuade him to hand over a monthly food allowance (no easy feat), half of which she'd give to Mae for groceries, with the rest deposited into the bank account of Mr. Wade Jordon, who ran a diner/gas station only a few miles from the farm. "If we pay up front for his weekday lunches," Mama said, "he'll be sure to show up." On Saturdays, which was the day when farmers came to town for supplies, Granddaddy would have lunch at our house, something simple like hot dogs or potpies. Then, following church on Sunday, Mae would take over Mawmaw's role and prepare a big family dinner for us all.

As Mae and Mama worked out the details, they joked about my grandfather's stinginess. "He's tighter than Jack Benny," laughed Mama. "It's those Scottish roots," chimed in Mae, who believed that any undesirable trait could be traced back to some kind of ethnic lineage.

I laughed along with them, but I'd never really thought of Granddaddy as a tightwad. Sure, he gave my brother and me only nickels when we'd run into him on Saturdays in town, while the Pruden relatives slipped us dollar bills practically every time they'd see us. But he'd bought me that Yankees uniform from the Sears Roebuck catalog, an act that had both amused and surprised my mother. For most of her life she'd known him as a hard, cold man who'd disciplined his children with a hickory stick—not as the kind and gentle soul who enjoyed baseball with his granddaughter.

Mama and Mae joked a bit more about Granddaddy's miserly ways. Then, as Ann and I joined them at the table, they began reminiscing about growing up with so little—the dolls made out of cornhusks, the quilts sewn from worn-out clothes, the feathered mattress where they cuddled together on cold winter nights.

"You don't know how good you two have it," Mama said, turning toward my cousin and me. As I gazed at the two seemingly different sisters, united by mutual pasts, I realized, perhaps for the very first time, that they were lucky to have each other.

15. Girlhood Dreams

The uniform was the best part of the job—the red-and-white-striped seersucker pinafore sewn by my aunt Mae, the short-sleeved white blouse with a Peter Pan collar, and the brand-new lace-up Keds. I liked the way the bib draped over my newly formed breasts and how the sash showed off my waistline. Except for the stripes not being blue and my hair being brown instead of red, I looked exactly like Sue Barton on the cover of *Sue Barton, Student Nurse.*

Earlier that summer, when Rosemary and I discovered the Sue Barton book series in the town library, we couldn't get enough of Sue's adventures in the nursing profession. It all sounded so exciting and glamorous, and we began to imagine ourselves earning caps just like Sue, working side-by-side to save lives at a large metropolitan hospital, and maybe even falling in love with handsome doctors.

Rosemary's father, Mr. Holmes, had come up with the idea of becoming candy stripers. "It'll be a good way for you to see what *real* nursing's all about," he told us. And since he was the rector of St. Paul's and often ministered to the sick, he had the connections at Chowan Hospital to arrange our one-week stint.

So there we were on that last Monday morning of school vacation, Rosemary and me sitting in the drab green reception room, dressed in our pinafores and ready to begin. We were all alone, for visiting hours were from five to eight p.m.—as noted on the sign above the hallway door, along with the words *No visitors age 12 or under*. I'd been there many times before, waiting with other children while Mama visited sick friends or relatives. Just that past year when Mama had a cyst removed, I was finally old enough to venture beyond its doors. I hadn't much cared for the smell of the place then—the antiseptic combination of alcohol and Lysol—and it still made me feel queasy.

To get my mind off my stomach, I looked at the picture hanging above the magazine stand. It was a close-up of a nurse, cap atop head and index finger pressed to her mouth to signify "quiet." With her pursed lips and intense stare, she looked nothing like Sue Barton. And neither did the mousy figure that suddenly appeared in the reception room doorway, clipboard in hand and a name badge telling us she was Mrs. Spiver, Head Nurse. As she looked Rosemary and me up and down from behind thick, winged glasses, she said she'd be our supervisor for the week.

Using a tone of voice that was as crisp as her starched white hat and uniform, Mrs. Spiver explained that since we were only fourteen and not skilled nurses or aides, our job was simply to offer the patients cheer and comfort—to chat with them, deliver magazines, and ask if they needed anything. Until we got the hang of things, we could make our rounds together. "And don't worry about the colored wing in the back of the building," she said. "They don't need candy stripers."

Rosemary led the way, entering each hospital room with a bounce to her step. "We're here to make you more comfortable!" she'd chirp as she fluffed pillows, straightened blankets, and poured fresh water—and I'd still be standing near the doorway, trying to get used to the sight of IV poles and urine bags.

On day two, when Mrs. Spiver asked Rosemary and me to split up after lunch, I was terrified to handle patients alone. My hands trembled as I poured cups of water, I was all thumbs with the pillows and bed linens, and my voice trembled as I tried to make conversation. When Rosemary and I switched sides of the hall after lunch, I could feel the patients' disappointment. "Where's the other girl?" one of them asked me, and I had to assure her that Rosemary would be back soon to check on her.

By the end of day three, I was becoming a little less ill at ease. Then on day four, Mrs. Spiver asked us to take on an additional responsibility. She was short on staff and needed our help with the call board, a panel of light bulbs behind the nurses' station, each one labeled with a room number and connected to a bedside switch. "When you see a bulb light up," she said, "go to the patient's room to find out what's the matter. If it's a medical situation, come back and get me. But if it's something simple, like needing water or a bedpan, you can take care of it yourselves."

Rosemary was thrilled with the new responsibilities—I could see it in her face—but I wasn't so sure. I cringed at the prospect of facing a serious medical situation, or even worse, having to help a patient with a bedpan. I wondered if Sue Barton ever had to empty bedpans.

When the first bulb lit up, Rosemary rushed to respond. "That's the spirit!" said Mrs. Spiver, and I took off in the opposite direction, hoping I could avoid the call board altogether. With the nurses' station right in the middle of the hallway, that was easier said than done—until I discovered the supply closet.

Approximately ten by twelve feet, it contained a large porcelain sink, a steel countertop, and shelves overflowing with Lysol bottles, Kotex pads, toilet paper, and a host of other hospital supplies in disarray. I began organizing them, making sure they were grouped together and in perfect alignment. Then I rearranged the soaps and bottles of Lubriderm lotion on the edge of the sink, taking my time and feeling more competent than I'd felt all week. I must have been at it for a good hour before Mrs. Spiver appeared in the closet doorway, hands on hips. "There you are!" she said, scowling at first, but then smiling primly when she saw the well-organized shelves. "Nice job," she said curtly, "but from now on, I want you to tend to patients, not supplies."

At home that night, Mama told me that Mag's former maid, Lucy, was at Chowan Hospital recovering from gallbladder surgery. She'd heard the news from Lucy's new employer, Miss Augusta Platt, who'd been in the bank that morning. "You might want to pop in to see her," she suggested. "I doubt she's getting much attention from Miss Augusta."

I hadn't seen Lucy since my great-aunt's death, and I was excited by the prospect of visiting her in the hospital. But then I wondered if Mrs. Spiver would allow me to go to the colored wing. Maybe it was better not to ask.

So the next day, after spending the morning with the white patients (who still didn't seem particularly happy to see me), I made my way to the colored women's ward at the far end of the hallway near the separate hospital entrance. Only a little bit larger than a double room in the white section, the ward was packed with six beds, lined up side by side with no curtains in between. And there was Lucy, eyes closed, in the one that was closest to the door.

If not for the name tag attached to her IV pole, I probably wouldn't have recognized her. During the past year and a half, her jet-black hair had become gray around the temples, and her dark-brown body, which was once so robust it practically spilled out of her maid's uniform, seemed almost lost inside the blue hospital gown. I unfolded one of the metal chairs stacked in the corner and took a seat beside her.

"Little Helen?" she asked, opening her eyes and then squinting as though trying to put me in focus. "Is that you?" Her voice was weak, but it was music to my ears—still smooth and resonant, as though coming from the center of her belly. "What in the name of Jesus are you doing back here in the colored ward?"

I explained that I was a candy striper and that Rosemary and I planned to become registered nurses like Sue Barton. Then as I gave my usual spiel about saving lives in a big city hospital and falling in love with handsome doctors, I noticed that my voice didn't sound quite as enthusiastic as it did at the beginning of the week.

Lucy studied my face for a moment as though taking it all in. Then she let out a deep, elongated *um-hummmm*—that same knowing sound she'd made when at age eleven I'd told her about my dream of becoming a major-league baseball player like Roger Maris. "Well, you do look mighty pretty in your little pinafore," she said. "There's no doubt about that!"

Eager to show her my candy striper skills, I began fluffing her pillows. "How was the operation?" I asked while clumsily tugging at her bedspread. And she told me it was a picnic compared to the terrible pains her gallstones had given her over the past few months. "If it wasn't for the money your great-aunt left me, I wouldn't be able to afford the surgery," she said. Then she went on and on about how kind Mag had been to her and how Miss Cornelia Plant, who had a reputation of going through new maids every few months, wasn't nearly as nice. "She was madder than a wet hen when I told her I needed to take a week off for surgery."

With that, Lucy began coughing. I instinctively reached for the glass of water on the bedside table and after only a few misses was able to hold the straw up to her lips. "If you don't mind, Little Helen," she said after a few sips, "I need to take a rest."

I settled back in the metal chair and watched as she dozed off. According to the clock on the wall, it was already a quarter past two, and my final candy-striping shift would end at three. If I stayed where I was, I could completely avoid the call board and bedpans—as well as Mrs. Spiver's constant scowl. Surely she wouldn't even think to look for me in the colored ward.

Lucy began snoring, and I smiled at the musical quality of her sounds—just being there next to her made me realize how much I'd missed her. She'd been one of the best parts of those Friday night dinners at Mag's house, and it seemed a shame that my great-aunt's death meant the end of our relationship. I gazed around the room at the other women, most of them sleeping, and

I wondered if they were all maids too. I began to feel angry that Miss Augusta Platt wasn't treating Lucy well.

I was still thinking about all those things twenty minutes later when Lucy opened her eyes. "Don't you have other patients to tend to?" she asked, looking surprised that I was still there.

"Oh, they're all doing just fine without me," I replied. "Rosemary's taking good care of 'em."

Lucy rolled over so we'd be face-to-face, her wise brown eyes looking right through mine. "Are you really sure you want to become a nurse, Little Helen?" she asked.

I think we both knew the answer.

At exactly three o'clock, when I approached the nurses' station to sign out one last time, Mrs. Spiver was chatting with Rosemary, who'd arrived there a few moments before me. "You were born to become a nurse," I heard her say. Then she turned my way and offered me a pen, not saying a word.

As Rosemary and I exited Chowan Hospital, leaving the antiseptic smells behind us, we talked about the new school year that would begin in a few days and made plans to see a movie that night at the Taylor Theater. But we didn't say a word about Sue Barton or working together in a large metropolitan hospital or marrying handsome doctors. I suppose we'd both realized that such dreams were no longer mutual. In only five days, Rosemary had found her calling in life, and I'd learned what mine wasn't. For now at least, I'd focus on a more immediate dream—becoming a John A. Holmes High School varsity cheerleader.

A WALK THROUGH THE VALLEY

(1966–1969)

16. Trials and Tribulations

Mama went into the hospital the same day cheerleader tryouts began. Probably just another cyst, she'd assured my brother and me—a simple procedure, just an overnight stay; there was a tuna noodle casserole in the refrigerator for our dinner. "See you during visiting hours," she'd said before we left for school.

Throughout the day, there were butterflies in my stomach—not because of Mama's operation, but because of tryouts. I knew I was a long shot to make the squad, since varsity cheerleading was the realm of upperclassmen and I was only a freshman. But leading parades up Broad Street and cheering the Edenton Aces on to victory had always been my dream. Why not give it a shot? What did I have to lose?

As I entered the girls' locker room after classes, I checked out the competition. There were a total of about twenty girls, all of them white, even though the school had become partially integrated the year before with four or five students from D. F. Walker assigned to each grade level (a half-hearted attempt by the all-white school board to obey federal law while at the same time stalling full-scale consolidation of the district's schools). And very few of them were sophomores or juniors—a good sign, because I'd be competing mainly with other freshmen for the five spots to be left open by graduating seniors.

Quickly I changed into my navy one-piece gym suit and joined Rosemary on the gymnasium bleachers, trying hard not to think of her as competition. During the nine years we'd been best friends, I'd always been the prettier one, as well as more athletic and more outgoing. But she'd blossomed over the past few months. The braces were gone, the pastel-blue glasses had been replaced by contact lenses, her all-arms, all-legs frame had suddenly become more womanly, and I was beginning to feel a bit jealous.

The head cheerleader, a graduating senior with a perfectly flipped hairdo and slightly bucked teeth, divided us alphabetically into groups of four, separating Rosemary and me. "We'll teach you a couple of cheers," she told us, "and then select the ten finalists who'll get to try out tomorrow in front of the coaches." I already knew most of the routines—I'd watched the squad closely during football and basketball games—but the butterflies wouldn't go away. I wondered if I was good enough for varsity cheerleading. What if Rosemary made the squad and I didn't? Would my voice crack from nervousness during my tryout?

When it was my turn to perform, I took a deep breath:

Give me an A! [arms up high]

Give me a C! [arms to the right]

Give me an E! [arms to the left]

Give me an S! [squat to the ground]

Whaddaya got? [jump up high]

Let's hear it again! [jump again]

One more time! [another jump]

YAY, ACES! [spread eagle]

My voice was clear and strong. I moved with precision and grace. I performed the routine perfectly. So did Rosemary during her turn. When it was announced at the end of the session that we'd both made the cut, we leapt to our feet and shrieked—paying no attention to the disappointed faces of the ten or so girls who wouldn't be back the following day.

"Let's go to Mitchener's and celebrate," I suggested as we skipped across the wooden floor to the girls' locker room to change back into our school clothes. It was only a little past four, leaving plenty of time for a Coke before Norfleet and I would go to the hospital for visiting hours. I couldn't wait to tell Mama my good news—she'd be so proud.

A few minutes later, as we crossed the front lawn of John A. Holmes High toward Broad Street, we spotted Mr. Holmes's tan Ford station wagon parked next to the curb. "He must be here to give us a lift," said Rosemary. As her father emerged from the car, all dressed up in his black shirt and clerical collar, she shouted, "We made the cut!"

Barely acknowledging our good news, he turned toward his daughter and said, "I'm here to take Helen to the hospital. I'll meet you back at the rectory." I was about to remind him that visiting hours wouldn't start for another half hour, that there was plenty of time for a Coke in town, but his uncharacteristically no-nonsense demeanor told me not to question his knowledge of hospital regulations. Rosemary flashed me a worried look before taking off down Broad Street.

During the five-minute drive to Chowan Hospital, Mr. Holmes offered no information about my mother's operation, and I suddenly felt too uneasy to ask questions. We only talked about the unusually cool May weather and the road construction along the way.

Once there, we silently walked through the drab green lobby, paying no attention to the sign that said *Visiting Hours, 5 to 8 p.m.*—or to Mrs. Spiver, who was seated at the nurses' station. As we made our way down the long hallway toward my mother's room, the familiar scents of alcohol and Lysol went straight to my belly.

Mama was sitting up in bed, wearing her own pale-blue nightgown and bed jacket rather than a hospital gown, and Norfleet and Mae were standing on each side of her. She smiled sadly when she saw me, and before I could even say hello, she got straight to the point. "I have cancer," she said, her voice cracking. "Tomorrow they're going to remove my breast."

I have only a vague recollection of what happened next—of holding my mother until it was time to leave, of the barely eaten tuna noodle casserole left on the kitchen counter, of Norfleet consoling me late into the evening. My next clear memory was of the alarm clock ringing at seven the next morning and my astonishment that it was humanly possible to stay awake for an entire night, crying and praying.

It wasn't a conscious decision to go to tryouts that afternoon—my body just took me there. There'd been no point in going home after school or to the hospital, where Mama was still in the recovery room. So there I was, emotionally and physically spent, seated with Rosemary and eight other girls on the bleachers, quietly waiting my turn. I was present, but not really there, paying little attention to the panel of coaches before me or to the detailed instructions given by the buck-toothed cheerleading chief. Rosemary had to nudge me when it was time for me to perform.

I rose to my feet and stood statue-like in the middle of the gymnasium floor—still so detached that I had to be asked twice to state my name and grade level. But when the head cheerleader snapped her fingers and shouted, "Please begin!" something deep inside of me ignited—as though a gigantic burst of energy had surged right through my veins.

We've got the Aces on our team—they're GRRRRRRRREAT! [clap, clap]

We've got the coach on our team—he's GRRRRRRREAT! [stomp, stomp]

We've got the spirit that a great team needs—it's GRRRRRREAT!

ACES! GREAT! [spread eagle]

Without even thinking about it, my words and movements were in perfect sync. My smile was radiant. My jump lifted me toward the rafters. I had conviction. I had school spirit. I performed the cheer perfectly.

"Very nice!" said Coach Kirby when I was done. "Please take a seat."

"We made it!" Rosemary shouted fifteen minutes later, when the new squad was finally announced. But I didn't really hear her. Alone on the edge of the bleachers, I was silently praying for a cure.

17. Hope, Prayer, and Cheerleading

One by one they came during visiting hours, a sisterhood of single-breasted women—the owner of Boswell's Restaurant, the treasurer of the St. Paul's vestry, the wife of a former mayor—women I'd never known had cancer. Each had her own tale of survival, her own message of hope. And as I listened in on whispered conversations about mastectomies, radiation, and prosthetic breasts, I began to believe that my mother would be just like them—that she'd be a survivor too.

Perhaps encouraged by those visits, Mama was surprisingly upbeat during the weeklong hospital stay. "How was your day?" she'd ask when Norfleet and I arrived each afternoon at five. And as we'd tell her about classes and school activities, she'd sip bourbon and water from a bent hospital straw. Of course alcoholic beverages weren't *officially* allowed at Chowan Hospital, but Dr. Williams thought a daily cocktail would do my mother good. A co-worker at the bank supplied the pint of Jim Beam, which was kept hidden from my aunt Mae and the nursing staff in a brown bag beneath the bed.

Once done talking about *our* day, we'd ask about hers. But she'd quickly reroute the conversation back to us. Were we keeping up our grades? Had the cheerleading squad chosen its new chief? Was Norfleet excited about graduation, less than a month away? "I should be healed enough by then," she said with conviction. "There's no way I'm going to miss graduation."

And with the help of her sister, she didn't. From the day Mama returned home from the hospital, Mae was at her side every day—changing dressings, helping her bathe, and organizing the platters of food dropped off by family and friends. Then on the night of the ceremony, she stopped by early to help Mama put on the short-sleeved, navy linen dress that had arrived from Lord & Taylor just before the surgery. "Thank goodness it fits!" Mama beamed as Mae easily pulled up the back zipper—but when she turned around and looked at herself in the mirror, her smile quickly dissolved. The bodice hung unevenly, for the "falsie" my aunt had sewn into Mama's petticoat the night before was at least a size smaller than the remaining breast, and my mother's right arm was so swollen with lymphatic fluid that it was nearly twice its normal size. Mae quickly reached for the large, white cardigan sweater hanging on the bedpost and draped it around my mother's shoulders. "Good thing we're not havin' a heat wave," Mama joked as we made our way out the front door, but it didn't really sound like she was joking.

Radiation therapy began the Monday after graduation, and it quickly took its toll. "How can something that's supposed to be so helpful make me feel so goddamn bad?" Mama complained after the first few treatments, which were now available in Elizabeth City, only thirty miles away. Mae drove her there several times a week, and when they returned in the late afternoon, Mama would go straight to bed. The radiation was not only making her weak, it also took away her appetite—so before leaving to take care of her own family, Mae would force Mama to take a few bites from the casseroles that were still arriving on our doorstep. Even so, I could see my mother's already slender frame becoming thinner and thinner each day.

"Losing weight is just a side effect of the treatment," she assured me, and I wanted to believe it was true—that she'd eventually gain it back and be healthy and cancer-free like the women who'd visited her in the hospital. But I'd hear the strain in her voice and see the fear in her eyes. And each night at bedtime my prayers became more intense. *Please, dear God, don't let Mama die like Daddy.*

Since making the squad in April, I'd been so preoccupied with Mama's health that I'd hardly thought about cheerleading. But now it was the end of June and time to begin our summer practice sessions, scheduled each Monday and Wednesday at two. Although the football team practiced at Hicks Field, located right next to the high school, the cheerleaders preferred meeting at the Courthouse Green, where the temperature was often cooler from the breezes off the bay. That suited me just fine, because our house was only a block away.

"Welcome to varsity cheerleading!" chirped Ann Harrell, the newly elected chief, as the rest of us formed a circle around her on the freshly mowed lawn. "Today's the day we start preparing for another exciting season of Edenton Aces football!" And with that, the squad's four veteran cheerleaders leapt into the air and shouted, "Go-o-o-o-o-o-o-o-o, Aces!"

"Go, Aces! Go, Aces! Go Aces!" chimed in the rest of the girls, and I had to force myself to shout along. Of course I *wanted* to be chirpy, for chirpiness was the mark of a good cheerleader, but enthusiasm that afternoon was hard for me to muster. Only an hour before, I'd accidentally seen my mother's bare chest as Mae helped her dress for the trip to Elizabeth City, and I couldn't get the image out of my mind. Its rawness had stunned me—the sunken chest cavity, the jagged surgical scars, the skin both inflamed and blackened. It had reminded me of a sun-scorched landscape, more dead than alive.

"Okay, squad!" Ann shouted, interrupting my somber thoughts. "It's time to line up and show me what you've got." She was only a slender five-foot-three and one of the sweetest girls at school, but in her new role as chief, she sounded bigger and less sweet.

We quickly arranged ourselves according to height, tallest in the middle and tapering down on each side, me second from the end next to Rosemary. Then Ann gave four snaps and three claps, our signal to begin:

Give me an A! [arms up high]

Give me a C! [arms to the right]

Give me an E! [arms to the left]

Give me an S! [squat to the ground]

Whaddaya got? [jump up high]

Let's hear it again! [jump again]

One more time! [another jump] *YAY, ACES!* [spread eagle]

As I yelled and jumped in sync with the other cheerleaders, my mind began to quiet and thoughts of my mother suddenly disappeared. My body moved with purpose. My voice was filled with joy. It was as though I'd been transported to a different place—one far away from worry and pain.

And that's how it was every Monday and Wednesday afternoon for the rest of the summer. Cheerleading became my escape. And perhaps it was my salvation.

18. Relief

Mama said there'd be a surprise waiting for me, and there she was—kneading dough at the kitchen counter, plump as ever in her starched gray-and-white maid's uniform, humming "Nobody Knows the Trouble I've Seen" or "His Eye Is on the Sparrow" (I don't remember which).

"Lucy!" I shouted while standing in the doorway. "What in the heck are *you* doing here?" I'd just returned home after one of the last cheerleading practices of the summer and was expecting to find a different kind of surprise—like a sweater from the Betty Shoppe for back-to-school, or perhaps a new book bag.

"I work here!" she said proudly. Then as I grabbed a Coke from the refrigerator and sat down at the kitchen table, she filled me in on what she'd been doing since I'd last seen her—that she'd returned to work too soon after gallbladder surgery the previous summer, and Miss Augusta Platt had fired her when the incision became so infected it required another hospital stay. "I was so happy when your Mama called," she sighed. "I sure did need a job."

Of course I was happy to see her and had no objections to her working for us, but I could feel a tightening in the pit of my stomach. We hadn't had a maid for several years now, not since Helen Austin moved north to be with her husband, and Norfleet and I were far too old for childcare. If Mama needed help, then maybe her radiation treatments hadn't been as successful as she'd let on.

"I'll be here only a few hours a day," Lucy said, as though sensing my worry, "just long enough to straighten up the house and cook y'all some supper."

I'd always enjoyed the weekly meals at my great-aunt Mag's house, and the prospect of eating Lucy's home cooking again made me smile. Nobody could fry tastier chicken, and her biscuits were so moist and flaky they didn't even need butter. "Well, you're gonna have to cook a lot," I warned, "'cause Norfleet eats like a horse!" He'd been going through a growth spurt over the summer—suddenly evolving from a skinny, pimply-faced high school graduate to a handsome six-footer about to leave for college.

"That don't bother me," Lucy chuckled. "I likes it when a man appreciates my cookin'."

Mama had been back at her job full-time for a few weeks now, and when she returned home later that afternoon, she was welcomed by the aromas of chicken fat, biscuits, and collard greens. "My goodness, Lucy!" she raved. "I think I've died and gone to heaven!" Although I cringed at her reference to death, I was glad to see her in such a good mood.

The previous day, she'd been so tired after work that she hardly ate a bite of the Dipsy Doodle hamburger loaf Miss Ruby Taylor dropped off earlier in the afternoon. Even though her radiation treatments were completed, Mama still didn't have much of an appetite for the one-dish meals we were still receiving on a regular basis. "If I never see another chicken supreme casserole or molded salmon ring," she'd said, "that's fine with me."

When we sat together in the dining room that night (not the kitchen, as we usually did), Mama ate like she hadn't eaten in months. She devoured an entire chicken thigh, two biscuits, two helpings of collard greens, a scoop of buttered rice, and a big slice of lemon pie for dessert. She ate almost as much as Norfleet, who was always ravenous after his summer job of mowing the lawn at St. Paul's. "Maybe I can gain back some of the weight I lost during treatment," she said, her voice sounding more robust than it had in weeks. "If anybody can fatten me up, it's Lucy!"

After supper, Mama watched TV with me instead of going straight to bed the way she'd been doing the past few months. And we were still in front of the television set, watching a rerun of *The Beverly Hillbillies,* when Norfleet returned from driving Lucy home. "You've already seen that episode," he reminded us. "Why don't we play a game of Scrabble instead?"

"You're on!" Mama shouted, which surprised me because even before the surgery, she'd rarely played games with us, almost always preferring to spend her evenings watching TV or doing the Sunday *New York Times* crossword puzzle.

Norfleet quickly set up the Scrabble board on the living room coffee table, and as we reached into the game box for our initial seven tiles, I told Mama that she could go first. She studied her tiles for a few moments before placing six of her letters onto the board—L, E, E, R, F, I. Then as she rearranged them to form the word RELIEF, she looked up at us and winked. "It sure is nice to have Lucy here with us, isn't it?"

"Yes, ma'am," I replied while tallying up her points (eighteen in all, double word score). "It sure as heck is!"

19. Missing Norfleet

The day had begun so joyfully, Mama getting up early to make pancakes and sausages, my brother's favorites, and taking the entire morning off so she'd be there to say goodbye when Mr. Holmes picked him up for the long drive to Chapel Hill. The kitchen practically overflowed with happiness—Mama beaming with pride; Norfleet so excited he could hardly eat; and me looking forward to being an only child for the first time in my life.

Of course I was proud of my brother, too. He was not only going to become a freshman at the University of North Carolina, a Tarheel, but also a Morehead Scholar, one of the chosen few white males in the state to be awarded full tuition, room and board, and even spending money. I was truly happy for him, but as a soon-to-be-sixteen-year-old who was in the habit of seeing somebody else's good fortune from my own point of view, I was even happier about what his departure would mean for me. There'd be no more negotiations over TV shows or music—I could watch *Bewitched* instead of *Star Trek* and listen to the Beach Boys on our new stereo rather than that nasally Bob Dylan whom Norfleet adored. There'd be no fights over the family car once I got my license in December. And best of all, there'd be no more competition for my mother's attention, not that I needed it much anymore.

As for his companionship, I no longer needed that either. Over the past year or two, we'd slowly grown apart, developing our own separate high school lives—his revolving around debate team, yearbook staff, and duties as senior class president; mine centered on glee club, the Future Homemakers of America, and of course cheerleading. Sure, his advice on which classes to take and which teachers to avoid was useful, and it was nice to get his help with difficult math problems. But the way I figured it, I could do just fine on my own.

When he drove me to school that morning, I was still in good spirits. "Good luck! Have a safe trip!" I shouted while hopping out of Mama's Fairlane. But then as I waved goodbye from the curbside, I was struck by a pang of melancholy that took me completely by surprise. It had come out of the blue like a dark thundercloud on a bright summer day, and it left me shaken and confused. Years later, I'd say it was the realization that my childhood was ending, that things would never be the same. But that's not what I thought about on that bright September morning. As I stood on the sidewalk in front of John A. Holmes High, my only concerns were the tears that were now rolling down my cheeks. Not wanting my friends to see them, I sneaked into the school's side entrance to the girls' restroom to wash my face before classes began.

Although I was no longer crying, I was still in such a funk

during first-period Biology that I could hardly pay attention to Mrs. Holiday's diagram of an amoeba on the blackboard. Mrs. Jenkins's second-period English lecture on the themes in *Great Expectations* went right over my head. And when my World History teacher, Mr. Bass, began describing the Peloponnesian Wars, he might as well have been speaking in Greek. Of course I knew deep down that Norfleet's departure had something to do with my lack of focus, but I refused to admit it as I slogged my way through the day.

It wasn't until sixth-period French that I finally got sick of feeling so *bleu. Pull yourself together*, I told myself. *Have a more positive attitude.* And that was when it came—an idea so brilliant, so *magnifique*, that I wondered why I hadn't come up with it sooner. Just thinking about it lifted my spirits, and I couldn't wait for class to end so I could hurry home to carry it out.

When the final school bell rang, I practically ran to my locker to gather my textbooks. "Wait up!" Rosemary yelled from behind. "Do you want to go for a Coke?" Since there was no cheerleading practice that afternoon, we were free to hang out with friends at the Mitchener's Pharmacy soda fountain.

"Not today," I replied while twirling my combination lock three times to the right. "There's something I have to do at home."

I made it there in less than fifteen minutes, not the twenty it usually took to walk the mile or so down Broad Street. The house was empty and the breakfast dishes were still in the drain next to the sink, because Mama had given Lucy the day off. So I plopped my books onto the kitchen table and hurried toward the rear of the house, passing through the tiny room where I'd slept for the past fifteen years.

When I got to Norfleet's bedroom, I paused for a moment in the doorway to take in all its grandeur. It was so much larger than mine—with windows on three sides and an attached porch that overlooked the bay. The only sound to be heard was the splashing of the tide on the breakwater just outside.

My room, in comparison, was downright noisy. Located on the side of the house that faced Broad Street, it was right across from the police station and the town sanitation department with its street sweepers and garbage trucks. It had only one small window, making it hotter than an oven in summer. And its view was hampered by an oil drum right outside and the backsides of Mr. Rhodes's shoe repair shop and the Chestnut Drycleaners, which when open for business spewed smelly steam. Being the second born, I'd clearly gotten stuck with the worst room in the house. But that was about to change.

I'd have to work fast to get the job done before Mama returned home from work. (She'd be so impressed by my initiative and industriousness!.) I scanned the entire space, doing a quick inventory. The furniture was fine—I could live with it. But those personal items would have to go.

I began with the wall décor. Down came the Boy Scout Troop 506 pennant and the Class of 1966 diploma. Next I removed the wall calendar with Civil War battle scenes and a portrait of Robert E. Lee. As for the "Go, Edenton Aces!" banner, I'd let it stay. After all, I was now a varsity cheerleader.

Next I attacked the large shelf that spanned one wall, removing all its contents and depositing them on the bed in my former room. It took several trips, as there was lots to carry—dozens of Landmark biographies, DC comic books, *Mad* magazines,

Norfleet's marble collection, his stamp collection, his rock collection, the plastic World War II soldiers he'd owned since age six, his pigskin football, the DAR Good Citizenship medal he'd won in eighth grade, his BB gun, and Teddy Roosevelt Pruden, the stuffed bear he'd cherished since age two. Before I knew it, my old pink gingham bedspread was piled high with relics from my brother's past.

When I returned to Norfleet's bedroom (rather, my *new* bedroom), I looked again at the space to determine what to do next. The contents of the closet and the chest of drawers could wait, and the white chenille bedspread could stay. But those curtains, the ones with cowboys and lassos and broncos—they'd have to be replaced. Something floral would look nice. Maybe I'd make them myself.

As I stood in the middle of the room, envisioning the dark-tan walls repainted a soft shade of pink and the empty shelves filled with my own personal knickknacks, the front door opened and closed. "Yoo-hoo!" Mama shouted, something she always did to announce her arrival. "Yoo-hoo!" I shouted back, which was my way of letting her know I was already home.

Clip-clop, clip-clop—I could hear her high-heeled footsteps coming toward me on the hardwood floors. But when they reached the tiny pass-through that was once my bedroom, the clopping abruptly stopped. "What in the hell?" Mama shouted. "What in the hell are Norfleet's things doing on your bed?"

"Oh, don't worry!" I shouted back. "I'll put it all away. I'm just switching rooms."

"You're *what*?" she demanded, now standing two feet in front of me, hands on hips.

"It's a much better room than mine," I explained, "and since he's not here anymore, there's no point in letting it go to waste."

Mama's lips tightened, her eyes bulged, and her face turned a bright shade of red.

"Your brother still lives here!" she screamed. "He's just away at college!"

Before I could say another word, she was sitting on top of the white chenille bedspread and sobbing her heart out. I didn't quite understand why she was so upset, but I reached for the Kleenex box next to the bed (one of the few remaining vestiges of my brother) and handed her a tissue. Then I sat down beside her—and for the first time that I can remember, I was more concerned about *her* well-being than about my own. "Don't worry, Mama," I said, squeezing her close. "I'll put everything back the way it was. My room is just fine."

Mama blew her nose and looked at me for a moment. "We'll figure something out," she sighed. "It's just that I'm really gonna miss him."

"Me too, Mama," I said, tears now running down my cheeks. "I'm really gonna miss him too."

20. Comfort

So there I was, stretched out in the double bed, grinning from ear to ear, the white chenille bedspread pulled up to my chin. Mama and I had reached a compromise earlier that evening. I could *sleep* in my brother's room, but I'd have to return to my own bedroom when he was home for weekends or vacations. As for all his things, I'd have to put them back where they belonged—but that could wait until the weekend. She'd help. Maybe there were some items that could be thrown away.

Since I'd never slept alone in a bed so large, I tried out all the options—first the right side, next the left, then settling on the middle, slightly catty-cornered. The peace and quiet were luxurious, the only sound being the tide lapping onto the breakwater—quite an improvement over street sweepers and police cars. I closed my eyes, ready to drift off to eight hours of uninterrupted sleep, when suddenly a venetian blind banged against the open window on the bay side of the room, causing me to sit upright in bed.

Just the wind, I told myself before lying back down and rolling over to face the wall.

... or maybe a Peeping Tom.

The thought of a stranger peering in at me sent a shiver down my spine. I pulled the bedspread over my head, but it did nothing to slow my racing heart. There'd been a rumor around town that a prowler was on the loose, and I wondered if it was true. I tried to calm myself by listening to the lapping tide, but even that was now more unsettling than soothing. I began to long for the familiar din of street sweepers and police cars.

Maybe I should return to my own room, I thought. *What prowler in his right mind would peek in from the side of the house across from the police station?* But then I remembered my bed was still piled high with Norfleet's things. It would take too long to remove them.

I placed a pillow on top of my already covered head. While it blocked out most of the sounds, I was now so wide awake that my imagination went wild. I envisioned the Peeping Tom standing outside the open window—his evil leer hidden by shadows, his hot, raspy breath camouflaged by the splashing of the tide.

I clutched the pillow closer, but my mind was now spinning with thoughts more real than imagined. Faster and faster they came, piling on top of each other. I thought about the next day's biology test and the pep rally scheduled for late afternoon and the terrible haircut I'd just gotten at the Nu-Curl Beauty Salon. Did I know what an amoeba looks like? Could I remember the new cheerleading routine? Would I have time to set and dry my hair before the pep rally?

The venetian blind banged once more against the open window, and as I again sat upright in bed, I was struck by a worry that made all the others seem trivial and small. *Did Mama's radiation treatments really work—was the cancer completely gone?*

I quickly rose to my feet and made my way down the hall toward my mother's room. I tiptoed across the floor to the empty twin bed where my father had slept before he died. I pulled down the covers and quietly crawled in.

"Are you okay?" Mama asked, looking up from her own bed just a few feet away. She sounded alarmed, for I slept in her room only when I was sick.

"I'm fine," I replied. "I just can't sleep."

"I can't either," she said, and I could see a smile emerge in the faint glow of the moonlight.

She settled back down. Then after a few moments, I heard her calm, rhythmic breath in concert with the rippling tide outside. I let my body melt into the mattress. Before I knew it, I, too, was drifting off to sleep.

21. Life Is Good

Thanks to Lucy's good cooking, Mama was getting stronger and gaining back some of the weight she'd lost during radiation therapy. She seemed happy to be back at work. And from Daddy's former bed, which was where I'd begun sleeping on a regular basis, I liked watching her get ready for it. When I'd wake up at seven each morning, she'd be sitting at the vanity—already bathed and dressed in her bra, girdle, and stockings beneath a blue silk bathrobe. "So what are you gonna wear to work today?" I'd ask sleepily.

"I'll let *you* decide" was her usual response. Then as she removed the hairnet and rubber-tipped bobby pins she'd slept in overnight, I'd crawl out of bed and select one of the pastel, short-sleeved shirtwaists that took up most of her closet. It was her favorite style of dress, and before the surgery, she'd stocked up on just about every color of the rainbow.

Once buttoned up and belted, she'd spray her wrists with Chanel No. 5, clip on a pair of earrings, and then drape the white cable-knit sweater around her shoulders like a shawl. "It's that damn air conditioning," she'd tell me, as though she needed an excuse for wanting to conceal her lopsided chest and swollen arm. "I think the bank is trying to freeze us all to death!"

When the People's Bank & Trust corporate office announced in early October that all female employees would be required to wear uniforms to work—navy wool skirts, white button-down shirts, and navy cardigans monogrammed with PB&T, I thought Mama would be happy to replace that old white cable-knit with a sweater provided by the bank. But I quickly learned I was wrong.

"They're taking away our freedom," she grumbled soon after hearing the news. "They're stifling our sense of style! I notice the male tellers aren't being asked to wear uniforms!" She ranted and raved for days, but when the uniforms arrived and she was handed a size 10, she wore it to work without complaint. I guess she realized she had no choice in the matter.

As a member of the varsity cheerleading squad, I, too, was required to wear a uniform; but to me, it represented privilege rather than constraint. In fact, I'd fully embraced just about everything related to cheerleading—the demands as well as the glory. There were two-hour practice sessions three days a week after school and pep rallies most Thursday nights. And then on Friday afternoons, before the big game, I had my own personal challenge—turning my coarse, unruly mane into the perfect cheerleader flip.

Beginning at the kitchen sink, I'd wash and rinse with Prell, followed by a healthy dose of Suave conditioner. Then, seated at Mama's vanity, I'd coat my hair, small sections at a time, with

Dippity-Do styling gel, roll each piece around a giant curler, and then bake under my portable GE hair dryer for forty-five minutes or more. Once dry, I'd remove the curlers, tease the hair on top, and then use my fingers to form one flipped-up curl extending from the bottom of one ear all the way around to the other. I'd have to work fast so I could lacquer it down with hair spray before it went awry. Then, ever so carefully, I'd lift the navy-blue cheerleading sweater over my head, making sure its giant "E" wasn't crooked.

"I think you spend more time on your hair than I do," Lucy said one Friday as she served me an early supper of grilled cheese and Campbell's tomato soup. "Maybe we should both just accept what the good Lord gave us." I looked at Lucy's perfectly coiffed pageboy and tried to imagine what she'd look like if she didn't make frequent trips to the Cut-rate Beauty Shop on Oakum Street, as most of the maids in town did, for chemical straightening and waxing. Would she look like Buckwheat on *Little Rascals*, who had hair sticking out every which away? And then I thought about my own hair, which in its natural state would be just about as unruly as Buckwheat's. "It's just something I have to do," I said with a sigh. "Nobody likes a frizzy-haired cheerleader."

One hour before kickoff, the atmosphere on the Courthouse Green was electric—the sounds of drums and tuning brass filling the cool night air, the townspeople gathering on each side of the street in anticipation, the police car flashing its lights to clear the parade route, and me so excited I could feel my heart beat. I'd quickly find my place in line with the rest of the squad. Then with three sharp toots from the drum major's whistle, the band would begin playing "On, You Aces" to the tune of "On, Wisconsin" as the John A. Holmes High School cheerleaders, with the majorettes right behind us, led the procession up Broad Street—all the while skipping to the beat of the drums, shaking our blue-and-gold pom-poms, and smiling at the adoring onlookers.

Once we reached Hicks Field, we'd make our way to the goalpost closest to the school where beneath the glow of Friday night lights, we'd stand at attention for the national anthem. Then, at exactly five minutes before kickoff, the drums would roll, the crowds would roar, and the John A. Holmes High varsity cheerleaders would race across the field with the mighty blue-and-gold football team right behind us. "*Goooooooooooo, Aces!*"

Positioned in front of the bleachers, we'd bounce and jump for the next couple of hours, shouting "Hold that line!" or "Go to the goalpost!" depending on who had the ball. If the Aces scored, we'd sing "Rah, Rah for Edenton!" to the tune of "Cheer, Cheer for Old Notre Dame." If the other team scored, we'd shout, "Block that kick! Block that kick!"

Throughout the game, I'd focus my attention on the student section in front of me, moving to the beat of the band and urging friends and classmates to join us in our cheers. When my cousin Henry (#82) did something great, I'd gaze at the section above, where Mae and Bill would be up on their feet, clapping and cheering for their son. Mama was usually there beside them, still in her PB&T sweater. But instead of watching the football game, her eyes would be only on me.

I'd raise my pom-poms in a subtle salute and leap even higher than before. For now, at least, life was good.

22. The Worst that Can Happen

The Aces won the conference football title. The holidays came and went. Then in mid-January, not long after Norfleet returned to Chapel Hill for second semester, Mama caught a cold. Not a serious one—just the kind of carry-a-Kleenex-with-you cold that most people tend to ignore. But it wouldn't go away, and after a few days of sniffling and sneezing, she arrived home from work feeling so tired and achy she could only pick at the chicken-fried steak Lucy made for supper. "I'm going to turn in early," she announced as she slowly rose from the table. And then for the first time since I'd gotten my driver's license the month before, she told me I could drive Lucy home that night, all by myself.

"Do you know the way?" Lucy asked a half hour later as she automatically climbed into the backseat of Mama's Fairlane, even though it was just the two of us.

"Of course I do!" I replied, for on those evenings when I didn't have to cheer at a game or attend a pep rally, I'd made the trip with Mama right there beside me on the front seat. All the way, she'd calmly given me directions: "Right on East Albemarle, left on Oakum," along with gentle admonitions like "slow down" or "turn off your right blinker."

So with hands placed precisely at ten and two o'clock on the steering wheel, I carefully made my way up Oakum Street, past D. F. Walker High, and toward Lucy's unpainted, ramshackle house in one of the colored sections of town. She lived there with her longtime boyfriend John Henry, which was about the only thing I knew about her personal life. I had no idea what her house looked like inside, or what she did for fun after work. Except for the blue cotton johnny she'd worn while a patient at Chowan Hospital, I'd seen her only in her maid's uniform.

She, on the other hand, knew just about all there was to know about me—who my friends were, how much soap I used in the shower, even when I was having my period since she was the one who emptied the bathroom wastebasket. That's just the way it was. Nearly half the town's population of five thousand lived in a colored section like Lucy's, yet I only really knew my own little world—the white-owned businesses on Broad Street, my barely integrated high school, and the well-kept neighborhoods of family and friends. As far as the white community was concerned, the colored sections were for dropping off and passing through, not for visiting. When the car was fifty yards from Lucy's house, I turned on the right blinker even though there were no other cars in sight. Then as I carefully pulled over onto the sandy gravel that served as a sidewalk, I put the car into park and turned toward the backseat. "Do you think Mama's gonna be okay?" I asked, even though my mother had assured me that a good night's sleep was all she needed.

Lucy slowly resealed the aluminum foil that covered the platter of leftovers she was bringing home for herself and John Henry. Then as she opened the car's back door and hoisted her ample body out, she finally answered, "Your mama's gonna be just fine, Little Helen." And I tried not to notice the hint of doubt in that deep, melodious voice.

The following morning, Mama's chest was so heavy with congestion she could hardly talk, so she had me call her boss, Mr. White, to tell him she was too sick to go to work. "I should be fine in a day or two," she rasped before I left for school.

But the congestion only got worse over the next couple of days, so Dr. Williams arranged for some tests at the hospital in Elizabeth City. Mae drove my mother there, just as she'd done for the radiation treatments five months before.

When I got home from school that Friday afternoon, they hadn't yet returned. I quickly did my hair and put on my cheerleading uniform, for I had to leave for the basketball game by six. "Don't worry about your mama," Lucy said as she served me an early supper. "I'll keep a plate warm for her." Assuming that what my mother had said earlier that morning was true, that she probably just had a bad case of the flu, I hurried off to the John A. Holmes High gym.

Mama was asleep when I returned home after the game, so I waited until the next morning to tell her about it. "We won!" I said first thing, before "Good morning" or "Are you feeling better?" or "How'd the tests go?" Then, as I began describing Wes Chesson's miraculous mid-court shot in the final seconds of play, I noticed she wasn't listening.

"What's the matter?" I asked, rising from my father's bed and taking a seat on the edge of hers. "Is everything okay?"

Mama was silent for a moment, and I began to feel uneasy. "I won't be going back to work," she said, a simple sentence that under different circumstances might have had a completely different meaning. But I knew exactly what she meant—I could see it in her eyes. "The cancer has spread to my liver," she said next. And by the third sentence, "There's nothing they can do," I was in her arms, weeping.

We both wept, holding each other tightly, me never wanting to let go—until she cleared her throat and gently pushed me away. "We can't fall apart like this," she whispered. "We have to stay strong." Then she reached for a tissue from the box next to the bed and slowly dried my tears.

Her sudden composure stunned me, and I cleared *my* throat, trying to follow her example. Then I asked a simple question: "What's gonna happen to me?"

Mama dried her own tears before speaking. "Both Lina and Mae have offered to give you a home when I'm gone. It's up to you to choose."

Of course, she didn't expect an immediate decision, but I answered right away. I didn't take the time to think about convenience (Lina's house was closer to friends and school). Or money (Lina was much better off financially). Or even religion (Mae and Bill were straightlaced Southern Baptists, while Lina was an Episcopalian like me). In truth, I didn't really think at all. I just knew deep down that with their sisterly bonds, Mae was the closest thing to Mama I'd ever find. "I'd rather live with Mae," I said. It was an answer that came straight from the heart.

Mama's tight, worried face began to soften. "That's who I hoped you'd choose," she said. Then she reached for the envelope on the edge of her bedside table and asked me to mail it right away. It was a letter addressed to my brother.

23. The Shadow of Death

Yea, though I walk through the valley of the shadow of death,
I will fear no evil: for thou art with me;
Thy rod and thy staff they comfort me. (Psalm 23:4)

I suppose it would have been liberating to accept the inevitability of death. There'd be no more worries about the cancer spreading; no more questioning of every sore throat, headache, or bump under the skin; and no more bargaining with God—*If you make Mama well, dear Lord, I'll never ask for anything else.* I'd just put one foot in front of the other, taking each day as it came, and try to be strong—like Mama.

But death was unacceptable, so I continued to cling to hope—checking the *News & Observer* each morning for news of a cure, praying at bedtime for a miracle, and refusing to believe that a gracious and loving God would be cruel enough to take my mother away. When friends at school asked, "How's your Mama?" I'd say she was doing fine. "And puttin' on weight!" I'd add, wanting to believe that the distended belly was from Lucy's good cooking and not because of the disease. Day after day, my answers were always the same, and after a while, friends no longer bothered to ask. I suppose there's no better silencer than denial.

If Mama was afraid of dying, she certainly didn't show it. In fact, she seemed strangely energized after the prognosis—making all kinds of arrangements and bossing everyone around. Mae came each morning at eight to help her bathe and make lunch. Lucy arrived at two to straighten the house and prepare the evening meal. Then on Tuesday and Friday nights, when I had to cheer at basketball games, Mae would return with Bill at seven to drive Lucy home and then visit until bedtime.

As for me, Mama had only a couple of requests—to keep my grades up and stay active at school, which was exactly what I tried to do. I maintained my straight-A average; I continued to cheer the Aces on to victory. "Just keep on doin' what you're doin'," she'd tell me—which must have been the same advice she'd given my brother.

On the day he received her letter, he'd skipped his afternoon classes and hopped onto the next Trailways bus heading east from Chapel Hill—a nearly five-hour trip that included layovers in Raleigh and Williamston, as well as stops at practically every crossroads and filling station along the way. When he arrived home late that evening, I was already asleep.

"Your brother has surprised us with a visit!" Mama announced the next morning. She was sitting up in bed and grinning from ear to ear as though the visit had nothing to do with her letter. I jumped out of bed to greet him, but Mama quickly stopped me. "He and I were up half the night talking," she said. "We should let him sleep."

I skipped cheerleading practice that afternoon, telling the chief I had a headache, so I could hurry straight home after school. There was so much I wanted to talk to Norfleet about—my fears, my sadness, my uncertainty about the future—things that only he could understand. All day long I'd envisioned the two of us driving out into the country to talk or perhaps taking a walk around the Courthouse Green.

"Where's Norfleet?" I asked when I entered the front door and found Mama alone on the living room sofa.

"I insisted that he go back," she said, barely looking up from her half-done crossword puzzle. "He's already missed enough classes."

I had to bite my tongue and struggle hard to keep from crying.

During the weeks that followed, Mama and I rarely discussed her illness. Instead, we talked about trivial things like the evening's TV lineup or what Lucy was cooking for supper. Or I'd amuse her with funny stories about school—like how the French teacher's new permanent wave made her look just like a poodle, or how during English class, Scott Harrell had farted right in the middle of Ronnie Rogerson's recitation of Marc Antony's eulogy to Julius Caesar. I'd often embellish my tales to make them even funnier, and sometimes we'd both be laughing so hard that I'd hardly notice her yellowed skin and distended belly.

But then there were days when I'd look into her sunken eyes and find it impossible to be witty. "I need to get a little fresh air," I'd say. "I'll be back in a few minutes." So I'd hurry outside, my heart in my throat, and cross the little historical plaza at the foot of Broad (the one with the single Revolutionary War cannon and the Confederate monument). I'd make my way toward the edge of the bay—all the while praying, *Please, dear Lord, give me strength.* Then as I'd take a seat on one of the breakwater pilings that lined the water's edge, I'd gaze at the scene before me—the soft light dancing on the rippling tide, the gray-green Spanish moss dangling from cypress trees, the late afternoon sky becoming soft shades of pink and lavender.

Sometimes the beauty and tranquility of it all would restore me. But most days I'd dissolve into tears.

24. The Pilgrimage

Spring came early that year, and from the looks of things, it was there to stay. Each day was warmer than the last, and the bulbs Mama planted the previous fall were now bright yellow daffodils, standing tall against the garden wall. It was the kind of blue-skied, bird-chirping spring that put a smile on people's faces—especially those of the organizers of the Edenton Pilgrimage, a biennial two-day event in which the town's historic public buildings and fine antebellum homes were open to visitors from far and wide.

As a member of the Edenton Women's Club, Mama had always been involved—mailing out flyers to other clubs throughout the state, making chicken salad for the kickoff luncheon, and manning an information booth on the Courthouse Green. But this year she could only hear about the event from friends who stopped by on their way to and from their planning meetings.

"I hear that Mulberry Hill Plantation will be on the tour this year," she told me after one of those visits. "I'd just love to see what the Woods have done to that place." But of course that wouldn't be possible, because she'd become so weak during the past couple of weeks she could hardly make it from her bed to the toilet. Lucy had begun preparing a tray for me each night so I could eat at Mama's bedside—not that either of us had much of an appetite those days.

Even so, just talking about the Pilgrimage seemed to perk Mama up. "I can't imagine two prettier tour guides!" she said when Mr. Holmes invited Rosemary and me to be the official hostesses at St. Paul's. "Tell me everything you learned," she'd demand after training sessions. And I'd sit on the edge of her bed and deliver my spiel about St. Paul's being the second-oldest parish in North Carolina and how the churchyard included the graves of a signer of the Declaration of Independence, a delegate to the Constitutional Convention, and the town's namesake, Charles Eden, the royal governor who was rumored to have been in cahoots with Blackbeard the Pirate.

Although it had been interesting to learn about the church and its history, Rosemary and I were even more excited about being excused from school on the first day of the Pilgrimage, a Friday. And to top things off, we could dress up in colonial costumes, just like the Women's Club and Daughters of the American Revolution ladies who served as hostesses at other historical sites around town. We'd already purchased patterns from Belk Tyler's, along with lavender calico fabric for matching dresses.

In Home Economics class, I'd learned to sew simple shifts and shirtwaists, but never anything as complicated as a colonial costume. So I set up my portable Singer sewing machine in

Mama's room so she could give me advice. "Make sure you pin the right sides together," she'd remind me from her bed, or "Baste before you stitch," or "Don't forget to press open the seams." And although her voice was weak and her breathing was becoming more labored every day, she'd spout off her orders with authority even though she knew as little as I did about the construction of eighteenth-century garments.

The project took much longer than expected, and the night before the Pilgrimage was to begin, I was still working on the finishing touches. "I can't wait to be done," I said as I pinned eyelet lace around the cuffs and neckline.

"Neither can I," Mama whispered, more to herself than to me—and I wouldn't let myself consider the possibility that she wasn't referring to the dress.

As I placed the fabric and lace beneath the presser foot and began to stitch, Mama told me about her day—how my aunt Lina had stopped by with the latest town gossip, which included news of the death of Mr. Halsey, the feed store owner down the street. I paused mid-seam, not quite sure how to respond, for we weren't in the habit of discussing bad news. Then, after a moment or two of silence she spoke again, her voice barely audible. "I hope I'll be next."

I carefully realigned the fabric and continued to stitch, acting as though I hadn't heard her.

25. Three Days in April

As soon as Mr. Holmes appeared in the doorway of St. Paul's, I knew why he had come. I could see it in his pale blue eyes—the way they scanned the clusters of tourists before falling upon me in my lavender colonial costume. From behind the metal-framed glasses, they radiated the kind of gentle consolation you'd expect from a minister bearing bad news.

I quickly finished my spiel on the parish's two-hundred-year history and followed him into the spring-filled churchyard—all the while taking no notice of the blossoming dogwoods or the bright pink azaleas that lined the rectory driveway. Instead, I focused only on his crisp, purposeful stride—each step bringing me closer to the moment I dreaded most.

Seated in the front of his tan Ford station wagon, I let only my ears absorb the moment—the low-pitched rumble of the engine, the tiny clicking sound of the left blinker, the uneven hum of traffic on Church Street—all wordless sounds that almost distracted me from my tightening stomach. Neither Mr. Holmes nor I spoke as we headed out Broad Street toward Chowan Hospital, where my mother had been since the day before when the bleeding began and the pain became so intense that only a morphine drip could help. "Go ahead to St. Paul's," Mae had told me that morning. "Your mama's resting comfortably; there's nothing you can do. Just stop by at the end of the day." Then as I turned to leave the hospital room, she'd added, "If she gets any worse, I'll send for you."

When Mr. Holmes drove by the hospital parking lot and didn't turn in, I wanted to believe I'd been mistaken. Maybe Mama was still sleeping soundly in her hospital bed, her condition unchanged, and he was simply giving me a roundabout ride home to be with Norfleet, who'd arrived from Chapel Hill the night before. Just thinking about the possibility made me feel better. But when we reached the end of Broad Street and I saw Mae's car parked in the driveway, the tightening quickly returned.

As we entered the front door, Norfleet and Mae rose silently from the living room sofa, their solemn faces saying it all. Then, as if on cue, Mr. Holmes placed his hand on my shoulder and whispered, "She's gone." The words just hung above me, and before I could react, he beckoned us to form a circle and pray for Mama's soul.

I stood erect with head bowed, unable to listen, unable to move—my body devoid of feeling. Then from out of nowhere came an unexpected jolt—a sensation that was so mighty and all-encompassing that it surged right through me. It lasted only a second or two, but when I eventually regained my equilibrium, I was left with a tranquility unlike anything I'd ever felt before. Years later I'd wonder if it was the spirit of my mother passing through me on her way to heaven—or perhaps God answering my prayer for strength, some sort of consolation prize after denying my pleas for a cure. But on that Saturday afternoon in April, I didn't think about either of those explanations. I only knew that what I'd felt was real and strangely empowering. By the time Mr. Holmes ended the prayer and we all said *amen*, I knew that everything would be okay. My greatest fear had just happened. Yet there I was, standing in the middle of the living room—still living and still breathing.

In a small town like Edenton, news of death travels quickly, so before I could change out of my colonial costume, relatives and friends were arriving with condolences and casseroles. Annie Mason, an aunt by marriage, was among the first. As soon as she walked through the door, she embraced me with her flabby, speckled arms. "You poor little thing!" she sobbed, holding me close, her frizzy red hair rubbing against my cheek—and all I wanted to do was release myself from her grip and get away from the sickeningly sweet scent of her Jergen's Lotion. I gazed over her shoulder at the other guests, hoping to be rescued. But when I saw only looks of pity, I pushed myself away. "I'm not a poor little thing!" I shouted as I retreated to my bedroom.

Once changed into shorts and a T-shirt, I stood before my window, trying to summon the will to reenter the living room and greet the visitors—knowing that's what Mama would have wanted me to do. But then I saw Rosemary in the distance, still in costume, rounding the corner and heading toward the house. I rushed outside to greet her, and as we embraced, I knew right then and there the difference between compassion and pity. "Come on," I said. "Let's get out of here!"

I don't know whose idea it was, but we somehow made our way to the St. Paul's Parish Hall rec room, where for most of the eleven years I'd known Rosemary, we'd played Ping-Pong whenever we were bored or restless or just needed an escape. Without speaking, we grabbed the two paddles left on the church school bookshelf and took our places at each end of the large green table that took up half the room. When Rosemary saw that I was ready, she put the ball in play.

Back and forth it went, rhythmically landing *kerplunk* on each side of the net, its contact with the table and our increased breathing the only sounds to be heard. Each rally was eternal, for our shots were steady and in control. Then all of a sudden, I uncharacteristically slammed the ball as hard as I could, sending it across the room, where it bounced off the wall before landing at Rosemary's feet. When she put it back in play, I swung even harder than before. As the ball ricocheted off the table's edge, Rosemary lunged for it, almost tripping on the hem of her lavender colonial dress.

"What does SHE know?" I shouted, finally breaking the silence and missing the return shot altogether. "I'm NOT a poor little thing!" Rosemary didn't know who I was talking about, but she didn't say a word. She just tried to return my increasingly erratic shots and listened as I channeled all my sorrow, all my rage, into one well-meaning aunt and a single plastic Ping-Pong ball.

When I was too exhausted to continue, I placed my paddle on top of the table and looked over at my friend. She, too, was exhausted, and the sight of her disheveled colonial hairdo and twisted crinoline skirt made me laugh. "I really do need to go back," I said. "People are gonna worry."

Rosemary accompanied me halfway home, and as I walked the final blocks alone, I worried about facing more hugs and kind words. Would I fly off the handle as I'd done with Annie Mason? Would I break down into tears? My emotions were in such flux, I had no idea what I'd do. Then, for no particular reason, I looked toward the Confederate monument that stood at the foot of Broad—and as I gazed up at the bronze-cast soldier, I found unlikely inspiration.

Champion of a lost cause, defiantly clinging to hope even at the bitter end, he wasn't that different from me. Yet there he was, appearing brave and strong, even in defeat. Couldn't I do the same? I'd already honed my acting skills—being cheerful at my mother's bedside, pretending to be optimistic when all I felt was dread. People expected me to become a defeated, grief-stricken orphan, but why couldn't I play a different role? Why not cling to the myth—just like the soldier? Maybe I couldn't become the musket-toting protector of "the land we love," but I could at least play the role of well-bred belle, the ever-charming hostess with a heart as tough as steel.

I entered the house with purpose. "You're so kind to stop by," I'd repeat over and over again. "We appreciate your sympathy." Gracious and poised, I offered tea and cake. I asked about children and grandchildren. I performed my role impeccably.

But when the last visitor left, so did my façade. As Norfleet and I emptied ashtrays and covered the many platters of food with foil, I began to cry for the first time that day—not yet from grief, but from feeling overwhelmed by the tasks at hand. "What's gonna become of the house?" I sobbed. "And Mama's things? And—and—and all this food?" I pointed to the stacks of casseroles that took up most of the kitchen table, and my shoulders began to quake. "It'll never fit into the refrigerator!"

Norfleet handed me a napkin from the box on the counter and placed his arm around me. "Don't worry, Little Sis," he said while holding me close. "Everything will be okay. We'll get through this."

I wiped my eyes and nodded. Of course we'd get through this. We had no other choice.

It felt strange not to be going to St. Paul's the next morning. As Norfleet and I made our way up Broad Street, there were no living things in sight—no shopkeepers, no leftover tourists from the two-day Pilgrimage, not even a stray dog. Most Edentonians, black or white, were inside their churches, and those who weren't would never be so bold as to appear in public during the hour set aside for Sunday worship. If not for our eleven o'clock appointment with the funeral director, we would have been in church too.

When we parked Mama's Fairlane in front of the Williford Funeral Home, Mae was already waiting for us beneath the canopied entrance. I'd never before been inside a funeral parlor, and as we entered the large front hallway, I was struck by the pungent aromas of musty oriental carpets, polished wood, and embalming fluid. I instinctively cupped my hand over my nose just as Mr. Bradley Williford, Jr. entered the room, hair greased back and dressed in a black tailored suit. "Please accept our sincere sympathy for your loss," he said—and as he extended his large, pasty hand to each of us, I was immediately put off by his well-rehearsed piety. *He hardly knew my mother*, I fumed to myself. *I'll bet he's just happy to get our business!*

After discussing the details of the next day's graveside service, he escorted us into a room filled with empty caskets, all of them, except for a pine box in the corner, opened so that we could see the plush interiors. He steered us toward the "Cadillac" model, with shiny brass hinges and made from the finest mahogany. "I can think of no finer way to glorify a loved one," he said while caressing the white velvet lining.

I cringed as I imagined Mama lying there in the rose-colored lace dress she'd set aside only a few weeks before. "Mama doesn't need to be glorified!" I shouted. "She's already in heaven!" Then, pointing toward the corner, I said, "Let's just put her body in the pine box."

Mr. Williford and Mae gasped in unison while Norfleet placed his hand on my shoulder to calm me. "Pine boxes are for poor whites and coloreds," Mae said gently. "Your mama deserves something better."

Eventually I agreed to a moderately priced casket, but I was still seething inside. When Mr. Williford invited us to come back at two for a viewing, I snapped, "I'd prefer for my last memory of Mama to be when she was alive." But that wasn't really the reason. Deep down, I was terrified that I'd crumble at the sight of her—and that I'd never be able to put the pieces back together again.

The following morning, Norfleet and I sat next to Mae and Granddaddy in the backseat of the funeral-home limousine as Mr. Williford drove us through the gates of Beaver Hill Cemetery. Pink and white dogwoods stood on each side of us beneath a sky of Carolina blue. But as we made our way down the dirt-and-gravel driveway, I could see only shades of black—the hearse in front of us and then the rows of mourners already gathered to bid my mother farewell.

I was not wearing black, but rather the navy linen dress Mama had ordered from Lord & Taylor before she got sick—she'd given it to me soon after becoming bedridden because, as she put it, "Good fashion shouldn't go to waste." My eyes were covered by large horn-rimmed sunglasses. They weren't necessary, as we were seated on fold-out chairs beneath a giant magnolia, but I kept them on anyway—in case there were tears to hide.

Breathe in, breathe out, I told myself as Mr. Holmes read from the Book of Common Prayer. *Just get through this; you can do it.* Instead of listening to the burial rites, I concentrated on my breath. Instead of watching the casket being lowered into the earth, I counted the trees beyond. *Breathe in, breathe out,* I repeated over and over again in my head. *Just get through this; you can do it. Don't fall apart.*

But no matter how much we prepare ourselves to be stoic and strong, it's often the unexpected that eventually makes its way through—that small gesture, that simple act of kindness, that genuine expression of regard. When the service ended and we made our way from the gravesite back to the waiting limo, I saw my classmates in the distance, gathered beneath a giant oak. They were supposed to be in third-period Geometry, and many of them didn't even know my mother. Yet there they were—for me. I lifted my hand to acknowledge them. Then as I settled into the limo's backseat and we headed out the cemetery gates, the tears began to form. Soon they were rolling down my cheeks—and not even my dark glasses could hide them.

26. Unexpected Consequences

At age sixteen, I suddenly had what most teenagers only dreamed of—a car, money, and popularity.

The car was Mama's Fairlane. "She wanted you to have it," Mae said after the funeral. "Norfleet can buy his own car in Chapel Hill." And although the intention was for me to be able to drive back and forth to school without having to depend on my aunt, I soon learned that having my own vehicle meant much more than transportation to school. As long as I returned when I said I would, I was free to go just about anywhere I pleased—to Sandy Point Beach for a swim with friends, to Elizabeth City to shop, or to Joe's Drive-in for a Coke or cherry soda after school rather than walk to Mitchener's, where the younger kids hung out. Then on Saturday nights, when most teenagers had to beg for use of the family car, I could cruise with my girlfriends up Broad Street, honking at boys in their borrowed cars, all the while relishing the privilege of ownership.

"Mag, from whom all blessings flow" was how Mama once referred to my late great-aunt, but until now I'd never known the full extent of those blessings. According to Mr. White, Mama's former boss and executor of her estate, Mag long ago set up trust funds for my brother and me for our health, education, and welfare. Mama had refused to tap into them—she wanted to provide for us on her own. So the assets had grown over the years, and there was now more than enough for my day-to-day expenses, college tuition, and anything else I might need. The trust, along with proceeds from the sale of our house and social security payments until I turned eighteen, meant there'd be no worries about me becoming a financial burden on Mae and Bill. But even more significant to me at the time was that I'd no longer have to rely on my Singer sewing machine to produce those front-tucked, back-zippered, A-line cotton print shirtwaists that were all the rage in 1967. With my generous monthly clothing allowance, I could now afford to buy *real* Villager and John Meyer dresses from Sawyer's Prep Shop in Elizabeth City.

Although Mae's fashion sense wasn't nearly as good as my mother's, I enjoyed having her accompany me on those after-school shopping trips. "How can anybody charge more than twenty-five dollars for a simple cotton dress?" she'd say as we flipped through the Prep Shop racks. But once I'd try something on, there'd be only words of praise. "That outfit looks like it was made for you," she'd rave, referring to the color, style, and fit—especially the hemline, which was usually an inch below my knees.

"Are you sure you want this halfway up to your wizmagog?" she asked me one afternoon after a shopping trip to Sawyer's. We were both in the center of her living room, me wearing my brand-new blue-and-white print Villager and her kneeling before me, straight pins held tightly between her lips, yardstick firmly planted on the carpet.

"It's the style," I said, slowly spinning around so she could line up the pins exactly twenty-six inches from the floor. And although she clearly didn't approve of my desired skirt length, she continued pinning and then offered to do the hemming herself later that night while watching TV with Bill.

The following morning when I dressed for school, anxious to show off my new outfit, I noticed that the finished hemline was an inch or so longer than I'd envisioned. "I had to allow for shrinkage," Mae explained sweetly when I asked her about it. "You know how cotton has a tendency to shrink."

"Yes, ma'am," I replied sweetly myself, for I had no desire to pick a fight with someone kind enough to give me a home. I'd just have to rip out Mae's stitching and re-hem the dress myself.

As for popularity, I'd always had a lot of friends; but during the weeks after Mama's death, I was lavished with attention. Boys who'd never noticed me before invited me out on dates. Girls asked to sit with me in the cafeteria. But the best thing of all was that I made the cheerleading squad again and was unanimously selected to be varsity chief for the coming school year. That meant I'd get to plan pep rallies, lead parades up Broad Street, even be interviewed by the local radio station. On the high school popularity scale, the position ranked right up there with starting quarterback. It was a dream job, and I couldn't wait to begin.

Football season was still months away, but I immediately called a meeting of the squad to discuss new uniforms—ones to replace the outdated knee-length skirts and bulky navy sweaters with their giant "E's" that did nothing to flatter our figures.

"What about navy dropped-waist jumpers with a white JAHHS monogram?" suggested one of the veteran cheerleaders as we gathered on the gymnasium bleachers after school. "Or maybe miniskirt and vests," offered Rosemary, my assistant chief. A couple of the newer girls liked the idea of blue-and-gold dresses, pointing out that those were the true school colors, not navy and white, the color combination traditionally worn by cheerleaders.

"Those are all great ideas," I said, trying to sound diplomatic even though I thought blue-and-gold dresses would be atrocious. Then I offered to meet with Mrs. Yates, the seamstress who lived across the highway from Mae, to get a cost estimate on the construction of each design. "That way we'll know how much money we'll need to raise before making a decision," I explained.

So later that afternoon I sprawled out on the bed in the room I now called my own and began sketching the designs on a sheet of onionskin paper, numbering them one, two, and three. *Which one would Mama like?* I wondered while shading them in with colored pencils. *She always said I looked good in jumpers.* Then, as I imagined her looking over my shoulder and offering her strong opinions, I began to cry—just a few tears at first, but then an outright bawl. Most days I could function just fine without her, but there were times like this when little things could set me off. I still missed her so much I could taste it—and I would have gladly given up the car, the money, and even cheerleading, just to have her near.

Pull yourself together, I told myself. *There's work to be done.* So I took a deep breath and wiped my eyes with my sleeve, just as Mae called from downstairs for me to help put supper on the table.

"What's the matter?" she asked when she saw my tear-stained face.

I walked over to the stove and began ladling the green beans into a serving dish. “It’s just my time of the month,” I said quietly. “I always get weepy when it’s my time of the month.”

In the foreground, the house Norfleet and I grew up in.

27. Moving On

He tried not to show it, but I knew it was painful for Norfleet to sort through his things. I could tell by the way he held each toy, picture, and knickknack a little too long, practically caressing them with his gaze. They all seemed to trigger long-buried thoughts of bygone days. "Remember when," he'd begin, and I would quickly cut him short.

"At this rate we'll never be done," I chided. "This is not the time to reminisce." Less than two months since Mama's death, Mr. White had found a buyer for our house. While Mae and I had already cleared out most of the rooms, we'd saved Norfleet's for his weeklong break between spring semester and summer school.

"You can't rush me," he said as he slowly sifted through the baseball cards he'd stored in a King Edward cigar box. "A lot of this stuff has sentimental value. I've got big decisions to make."

We'd been at it since early afternoon, and the only decision he'd made so far was to donate his Landmark biographies to the town library, and even that had been a tough one. "These books helped shape me," he'd said. "Suppose I have a son who wants to learn about Daniel Boone or Charles Lindbergh?"

"Just take him to the library!" I'd snapped, finally losing my patience.

To make things easier for him, I'd labeled three corners of the room with cardboard signs—one for items to store, one for those he'd take with him, and the other for things to get rid of. But so far the only visible progress was in the corner I hadn't labeled—the one Norfleet called "undecided."

I suppose I really shouldn't have been so hard on my brother. Unlike him, I'd been able to clear out my room gradually, bringing only toiletries and a change of clothes with me that first night at Mae and Bill's house. During the days that followed, I'd gathered more and more of my things until by the end of the week, my cousin Ann's room had been transformed into my own. Her closet and chest of drawers, which she'd emptied when she left for college, now contained only my clothing. Photographs of Norfleet and Mama sat on the windowsill, and my textbooks and Nancy Drew mysteries took up part of the empty bookshelf. The only vestiges of Ann were the high school diploma and graduation picture that hung in a double frame above the bureau. Otherwise, the room looked completely like my own.

Norfleet, on the other hand, would become somewhat of a vagabond. Of course, he was always welcome at Mae and Bill's, where he could share a bedroom with our cousin Henry, who was a year older than me. But it would never be his home. Instead, he'd use his brand-new metallic-blue Pontiac Le Mans as his base, storing essentials in the trunk and then moving them from dorm to frat house to apartment and then to wherever else he'd be. No wonder he was having a hard time making decisions.

It was well after three when he opened his closet door to an avalanche of clothing, toys, and sports equipment. "I've gotta go," I said, suddenly remembering I'd called for a brief cheerleading practice on the Courthouse Green. "Maybe you'll get more done if I'm not here to browbeat you."

"I'll do my best, boss!" he said with a mock salute.

When I returned an hour or so later, I was amazed by his progress. The bookshelf was bare, the closet was empty, and the pile in the "Undecided" corner was almost nonexistent. Most of the items in the "To Be Stored" corner were already neatly packed in cardboard boxes, and the "Get Rid Of" pile took up almost half the room.

I was about to praise him for his decisiveness when I noticed his old Louisville Slugger baseball bat poking out of the "Get Rid Of" pile. "Why do you want to get rid of this?" I shouted, almost causing another avalanche as I pulled it from the pile of broken toys, outgrown clothing, and the Landmark books that would go to the town library. "It's etched with Roger Maris's autograph!"

"You can have it if you want," he said matter-of-factly. "It means nothing to me."

Nothing to me. The words cut right through me. Clearly, Norfleet had outgrown the bat. And sure, the Yankees, his favorite team, had just traded Maris to the St. Louis Cardinals. But how could it mean nothing? Only a few years before, that bat had been our bond. It represented the many hours we spent together in the backyard, him pitching and me hitting. If anything were to be of sentimental value to him, it should have been the Louisville Slugger.

I just glared at him for a moment as he methodically continued packing the cardboard boxes. He'd changed so much during the past year. His six-foot frame had filled out so that he was no longer lanky. His thick, dark hair now covered his larger-than-average ears. He'd been such a goody-goody during high school, but over the past year he'd taken up smoking and drinking, and he now carried himself with the swagger of a Delta Kappa Epsilon frat boy. Even before Mama's death, it was clear to me that he'd discovered a new life in Chapel Hill that was far more exciting than the one we shared in Edenton. Of course he'd returned often, especially after Mama's health deteriorated, but deep down I knew that those visits were motivated by concern about our mother rather than a desire to be with me.

And as much as I wanted to believe otherwise, I knew it was duty that had brought him back to Edenton those past few days. I don't doubt he was happy to see me. But from overheard conversations, I also knew he'd prefer spending his break with fraternity brothers at Nags Head. "Don't have too much fun without me!" I'd heard him say on Mae's telephone. "If I'm lucky, I'll be out of here in a couple of days."

Holding tightly onto the bat, I watched him tape the last "To Be Stored" box shut. Then, as he began to fold the clothing he'd be taking with him, it occurred to me that with the sale of the house, our mutual lives would be over. There'd be no more homecomings, no more card games on the back porch, no longer a common place to jog childhood memories.

"I guess our days of playing baseball together are over," I said curtly, feeling a combination of anger and sadness.

He paused for a moment, as though surprised by my shift in tone. Then he walked over to me and placed his arm around my shoulder. "I guess they are, Little Sis," he said tenderly. "I suppose it's time to move on."

I pushed myself away, in no mood for his affection. "We need to finish up," I snapped. "Mae expects us to be at the dinner table by five forty-five sharp."

I returned the bat to the "Get Rid Of" pile, and we began loading the packed items into the trunk and backseat of the Le Mans. We worked in silence—Norfleet hardly acknowledging me, as though his mind was in a different place; me feeling as though my heart was about to break.

When the car was packed and we finally pulled out of the driveway, I focused only on the dash and the road in front of us. I didn't look back. Without my mother and brother there, the house meant nothing to me.

28. Another April

It was an unusually warm spring evening, even for eastern North Carolina with its predictably erratic April weather (85 degrees and sunny one day, a rainy 50 the next). While Mae and I cleaned up the kitchen after a simple supper of ham, potato salad, and sliced tomatoes, my cousin Henry, now a senior, headed upstairs to study for a physics test, and Bill settled onto the front-porch glider to listen to classical music on his transistor radio. Once done with our chores, Mae joined Bill on the porch and I began clearing a space on the living room floor for my nightly calisthenics. Since Mama's death the previous April, I'd gradually put on nearly ten pounds—weight I'd hardly been aware of until Norfleet referred to me as his "chubby little sister" during a recent visit. When Mae confirmed that I was indeed becoming a bit pudgy, I'd immediately started counting calories and doing a regular regimen of squat-thrusts, toe-touches, and sit-ups, in hopes of slimming down by the time the cheerleaders began summer practice.

With the Brandenburg Concerto wafting through the open window, I tried to sync my movements to the steady cadences of Bach—*one, two, three, four … bend, jump, squat, stand.* By the fifth repetition, I was already dripping with perspiration, so I stopped for a moment to wipe my forehead with the hem of my T-shirt. Then as I began a set of fifty sit-ups, the music suddenly stopped and the urgent-sounding voice of a newscaster blared from the transistor radio. I couldn't quite make out what he was saying—only the words *Martin Luther King, Memphis,* and *gunshots.* Within seconds, Mae appeared before me, looking worried and pale. "Martin Luther King has been murdered," she said solemnly, "and the nigras have already started goin' wild."

As she and Bill hurried into to the den to follow the developing news on TV, I tried to resume my routine, but I was much too shaken to concentrate. Unlike my aunt and uncle, who'd never particularly cared for Martin Luther King, I'd grown to admire him over the years—ever since his visit to Edenton right after I'd turned twelve. He'd come to encourage local black leaders in their campaign to integrate public facilities. Although few whites even knew he was in town, my brother had learned at school from the mayor's son that King would be speaking that night at the National Guard Armory. Hoping to get a glimpse of him, Norfleet convinced Mama to drive by the Armory after supper. "My goodness!" Mama had said when we saw the hundreds of people lined up at the building's front entrance. "I think every colored in the county has gathered here tonight. I wonder if they'll all fit inside." I now wondered how such a peace-loving minister could be murdered—and how my aunt and uncle could be more concerned about the aftermath of the assassination than the shooting itself. I slowly moved the living room furniture back to its original position and joined them in front of the TV.

The following morning there was a brief moment of silence for Reverend King following homeroom announcements. Then it was like any other Friday at school. After classes, I went with friends to Joe's Drive-In and ordered a Tab rather than a cherry Coke with Twinkies, which had been my usual after-school snack before the diet. With thoughts of the assassination now far from my seventeen-year-old mind, I arrived home at a quarter past four to find my aunt unloading bags of groceries from the trunk of her car. "Ann and Ken should be here in a couple of hours!" she exclaimed when she saw me. "Their school was let out early because of all the rioting."

Although I'd seen the TV news coverage of looting and fires in Washington, I was surprised that my cousin would be seeking refuge in Edenton. Since beginning a teaching job in a Maryland suburb the previous August, she'd rarely returned home—only once in December to introduce us to the high school coach she'd been dating, and again in February when she married him. For her and Ken to be making the nearly six-hour drive south, the rioting must have gotten pretty bad.

Despite the circumstances, Mae seemed excited about the visit. "I'm gonna bake Ann an upside-down cake," she said as she lifted a can of Dole pineapple from one of the many grocery bags we'd placed on the kitchen counter. "It's always been one of her favorites." And from the looks of things, Mae would be making *all* of Ann's favorites. She'd bought chicken legs, a ten-pound turkey, a roast beef, two boxes of Jell-O, whipping cream, four different kinds of vegetables, bananas, vanilla wafers, and a gallon of fudge ripple ice cream. It was clearly going to be a struggle over the next few days to maintain my 1,200-calorie diet.

"Don't worry about feeding us on Sunday," Ann said when we all sat down for supper after her arrival. During the drive down, she'd heard on the radio that a curfew had been imposed on the entire D.C. area, which meant that she and Ken would need to leave by noon on Sunday in order to be home before dark. Mae looked disappointed. "Well, we'll just have to have Sunday dinner on Saturday," she said with forced cheerfulness. "I'll give Papa a call right away."

And what a dinner it was—roasted turkey with dressing, sweet potatoes, green beans, lime Jell-O mold, and banana pudding with whipped cream for dessert. I took only a few spoonfuls of everything, just like Granddaddy, who was seated beside me—but unlike me, he wasn't dieting. Ever since my grandmother's death three years before, he'd had little appetite for anything. Except for weekly meals at Mae's house, he seemed to prefer being alone on the farm—watching TV from his vinyl-covered La-Z-Boy or just sitting by himself on the front-porch swing. We'd barely finished our banana pudding when he rose from the table and announced it was time to go home. "You have a safe trip back up to Washington," he said to my cousin. "And try to stay away from all those crazy, riotin' niggers."

The following day was not a typical Sunday. Mae and Bill skipped services at Edenton Baptist so they could bid farewell to Ann and Ken. Henry was spending the day with his girlfriend. And since there was no big family dinner to go to, I had lunch with Rosemary at the rectory after services at St. Paul's. I'd just returned home when Norfleet called to say he'd be passing through Edenton on his way back to Chapel Hill. He and his roommate, Caldwell, had spent the weekend at Nags Head in hopes of lining up summer jobs. But President Johnson had called for a national day of mourning, and all the businesses they wanted to contact were now closed. "I'm so glad they'll have time to stop by for a visit!" Mae said when I told her. "They can help us eat that big rib roast I bought on Friday."

When my brother's blue Le Mans eventually pulled into Mae's driveway, the roast was in the oven and I was upstairs, teasing and spraying my hair. As I watched the boys get out of the car from my bedroom window, I could see that Caldwell was just as cute as the dozen or so fraternity brothers who'd been at Mama's funeral the previous April. I quickly checked my flip in the mirror and applied another coat of hot-pink lip gloss before heading downstairs to meet him.

There were hugs from Mae and handshakes from Bill, and I was just about to say "How do you do?" to Caldwell when the telephone rang and Mae scurried across the living room to answer it. "Oh, my God!" we heard her cry as we stood awkwardly in the entryway, awaiting what was sure to be bad news.

"Papa died in his sleep," Mae said after hanging up the phone. "Willie just found him a few minutes ago."

"Oh, no!" we cried in unison. Then I embraced my aunt and offered the same empty condolence I'd heard so many times before: "It's for the best."

Caldwell looked at me with astonishment, and even I was surprised by my lack of emotion. There'd been so many losses over the past eleven years—Daddy, Mag, Mawmaw, Mama, my grandmother Pruden, and now Granddaddy. Could it be that I'd finally reached the point where news of a family death no longer stunned me? "He's now with Mawmaw," I quickly added, in an attempt to sound less callous.

As she did with most family crises, Mae immediately sprang into action. She and Bill would be joining my uncle Willie on the farm, so she quickly said her goodbyes to the boys. "Be sure to take some sandwiches with you back to Chapel Hill," she told them. "The roast should be done in a few minutes." And with that, she gave me a look that let me know I'd be left in charge of it.

With two years of Home Economics under my belt, I was an expert at making meatloaf and macaroni and cheese, but never before had I been responsible for anything as important as a roast beef. "How will I know it's ready?" I asked nervously.

"Just look at the juices in the bottom of the pan," she replied before leaving. "They should be a nice shade of brown, not red. But be careful not to overcook the meat. You don't want it to end up tastin' like leather."

Ten minutes later, with visions of impressing Caldwell with a perfectly cooked roast, I slowly opened the oven door. Were the juices a nice shade of brown, but not red? Maybe. Was it time to remove the roast from the oven? I figured a few more minutes wouldn't hurt. Of course, if Mae had owned a meat thermometer, my task would have been much less daunting. She was the kind of cook who relied on instinct, not science—just like Mawmaw. I wasn't sure if I'd inherited those instincts.

So I stood before the kitchen stove and worried. Martin Luther King had been killed only three days before. America's cities were erupting with rage. And the grandfather I'd always adored was now dead. But all I could manage to think about was not ruining the roast beef.

29. The Yoke of Duty

When my grandmother Madam passed away four months after my mother, it was considered by many to be a blessing. For five long years, since falling and breaking both hips at the age of eighty-five, she'd been immobile, bedridden, and on a slow decline. Although at first she'd tried to carry on from a wheelchair—telling Lillie exactly what to cook for supper, demanding that my uncle George include no more than three ice cubes in her daily cocktail of bourbon and soda, and insisting that Camilla, her hairdresser, stop by at least once a month to touch up her roots—Madam's body eventually weakened, as well as her need to control.

From the time I'd turned thirteen, my only image of my formerly outspoken grandmother had been one of a docile old woman lying helplessly in bed—a catheter extending from her bladder to a plastic pouch (which was always half-filled with urine), her thinning hair completely white (which Mama had said made her look kinder and gentler than when she colored her hair with henna), and with round-the-clock care, primarily by my aunt Lina, who long before the fall had given up a teaching career to tend to the needs of her mother.

After spending most of their married life as a threesome, it seemed natural that things would change for Lina and George during the year after Madam's death—that they'd redo the house to make it their own and resume their annual vacations to the Blue Ridge Mountains. But except for George retiring from his highway engineering job and taking up golf to fill the time, their lives stayed pretty much the same. Lina continued going to DAR meetings, they both remained active at St. Paul's (she in the altar guild, he in the vestry), and they still had me over for a once-a-week meal.

"Would you like ginger ale or a glass of sherry?" Lina shouted one August afternoon from the dining room tea cart, which, as always, was stocked with liquor, a few soft drinks, and a half-filled silver ice bucket with matching tongs at its side. Normally, George played the role of bartender, but I was there for lunch, not dinner, and he was off playing golf with Dr. Williams at the newly established Chowan Country Club, as he now did most Saturdays in summer.

"I'll have a ginger ale," I replied, not wanting Mae to smell alcohol on my breath when I returned home later that day. Even though I was still a few months shy of the legal drinking age of eighteen, I'd sometimes have a glass of sherry with Lina or a beer with friends. But it was always in the evening, when I could sneak upstairs to bed undetected by my teetotaling aunt Mae and uncle Bill.

"On the rocks or straight up?" Lina asked, her voice as lilting and high-pitched as ever.

"On the rocks!" I shouted while gazing around the living room from the red velvet sofa. I'd sat in that same spot nearly every Saturday for as long I as could remember, but I'd never before taken much notice of the surroundings—the heavy mahogany furnishings and musty oriental carpets dating back to the early 1900s, the portrait of my stern-faced great-grandfather hanging above the marble fireplace, and the knickknacks still sitting exactly where my grandmother had placed them many years before. For some reason, the sameness of it all now bothered me. When my eyes eventually landed on the rose-topped Limoges porcelain box that had always been on the coffee table, I impulsively picked it up and placed it on top of the baby grand—anything to change things up a bit.

"So are you excited about starting your senior year in a couple of weeks?" Lina asked while handing me my ginger ale and settling next to me on the sofa.

"Yes, ma'am, I am!" I replied, even though I was more excited about *finishing* senior year.

It wasn't that I didn't enjoy high school. I loved all my friends and was looking forward to being chief cheerleader for the second year in a row. And it wasn't that I didn't like living with Mae and Bill; they were nothing but kind to me. The problem was that I'd been having bouts of restlessness lately. When Norfleet called from Chapel Hill each Sunday night, I'd listen to his descriptions of rock concerts, antiwar demonstrations, and interesting people he'd met on campus, and my life, in comparison, would feel predictable and small. As much as I loved Edenton and the people who lived there, I'd begun to imagine being in a bigger place—maybe some faraway city like New York or Boston where no one knew of my loss.

"Before you know it, you'll be leaving for college," Lina said, as though sensing my restlessness. Then she launched into her usual monologue about being among the first ninety coeds to transfer to Carolina, and how she'd been a founding member of the campus's Pi Beta Phi sorority and had once danced with Thomas Wolfe, a fellow student. I'd heard the stories many times before and could probably recite them by heart, but I smiled politely as though hearing them for the very first time. I'd occasionally say "um-hum" or "oh-ho" to let her know I was listening. Then, as the china clock on the mantel struck one, Lillie appeared before us, all dressed up in her gray-and-white maid's uniform and ready to "pronounce" lunch.

The malapropism had been a family joke for decades, beginning when Lina and my father were children and Lillie was just a young girl coming to work each day with her mother, who worked as Madam's cook. Along with helping out in the kitchen, Lillie had been in charge of telling the family when it was time to come to the table—always asking my grandmother beforehand if she could "pronounce" the meal. She'd continue to work in the household long after her own mother passed away, but now she posed the question to my aunt instead of Madam. "Miss Lina," she asked with the right amount of deference, "is it all right for me to pronounce lunch now?"

As Lillie spoke, I thought about how so many of the town's well-to-do whites referred to their black maids as "just like family," a claim Lina would surely make about Lillie after so many years together. I'm not sure why—maybe because I'd been moved by

To Kill a Mockingbird in English class or because I'd recently seen movies like *Guess Who's Coming to Dinner* and *Hurry, Sundown*—but I was beginning to see hypocrisy in such assertions. Family members don't wait in the kitchen for leftovers after serving their "loved ones" a meal. They don't get paid less than a living wage for unconditional devotion. And they don't simply disappear from your life when their services are no longer needed.

Vanzula had cared for me like one of her own throughout my preschool years, but I never again saw her after Mama fired her for drinking on the job. Helen Austin, as far as I knew, was still living somewhere up north. And although Lucy was now working for someone near Broad Street, I'd run into her only once during the sixteen months since Mama's death. It was in front of the P&Q Market one afternoon after Mae and I finished shopping for groceries. "Lucy, I'm so glad to see you!" I'd shouted as I ran to her and embraced her. Then as I inquired about her health and new job, Mae interrupted. "We need to get the ice cream home before it melts," she said politely—but during the drive home, her tone was a bit less sweet. According to the aunt who'd never had a maid she could refer to as "just like family," it was inappropriate for a girl my age to embrace a colored person out in public. "Folks might think you're a nigger-lover," she told me. *Maybe I am,* I'd thought to myself. *Maybe I am.*

After Lillie's "pronouncement" of lunch, I took my usual seat at the dining room table as Lina shifted the conversation from college to "the news," a term she like to use for gossip. Being so active in the church and the local DAR, she knew just about everything going on in town—who was away on vacation, who was sick or in the hospital, who was here visiting relatives, even what people had for dinner. As she went on and on about this and that, I nodded politely, counting the minutes until I could return to Mae's house and sunbathe by the creek.

"You'll never guess who came to our DAR meeting yesterday," Lina said as Lillie removed our dinner plates and replaced them with her usual dessert of patty shells filled with applesauce and cream.

"Who?" I asked, not really interested in the answer but willing to keep the conversation going until the end of the meal.

"Elizabeth Cranmore," she said. "Can you imagine that?" Then as I dug into my applesauce, she explained that Elizabeth, who'd been working as a librarian in Raleigh for the past twenty years, had just returned to Edenton to take care of her ailing mother. "Oh, how I wish I had a daughter who could look after me like that!"

I had no idea who Lina was talking about, and I really didn't care. But as she spoke, I was suddenly struck by a thought that was so callous, selfish, and un-Christian that it took my breath away. *Thank God I chose to live with Mae instead of Lina, because Lina would expect me to stay here and take care of her—just as she'd done for Madam.*

I put down my fork, unable to swallow, before being struck by another thought that was even more startling than the last. *With no parental ties to Edenton, I'm free to live my life however and wherever I choose.* The realization was both terrifying and exhilarating.

30. Senior Year

Peaceful little Edenton seemed far removed from the turmoil that would characterize 1968, the year I became a senior at John A. Holmes High. Amid cries of "Black Power" and "Burn, baby, burn" in major cities during the months following King's assassination, town officials and local NAACP leaders worked quietly with the courts on a plan to finally consolidate the district's black and white public schools. While students at Duke and Carolina spoke out about the increasing number of casualties in Viet Nam, few white Edentonians were even aware of the loss of a native son, for his death notice had been buried in the "Colored News" section of the *Chowan Herald*. And as the Democratic Party reeled from rioting outside the convention in Chicago that summer, a majority of Chowan County's voters abandoned their party allegiance for the first time since before the Civil War and supported the third-party presidential candidacy of the segregationist governor from Alabama.

"But he's so hateful and mean-spirited," I complained as I took a seat at the kitchen table, which was where we'd begun having dinner each night since my cousin Henry's recent departure for college. "How could anybody with any decency support Wallace?" As the newly appointed Democratic chairman for the upcoming mock election at school, I'd been shocked by the number of "George Wallace for President" posters already covering the gymnasium wall. There'd been barely enough space for the five red and blue Magic-Markered "Vote for Hubert Humphrey" signs my committee of five had worked on so painstakingly all afternoon.

"Well, at least he's someone who'll stand up for law and order," Bill replied as he dished out the meatloaf Mae had placed before him. "Under the Democrats, we sure wouldn't get much of that."

"But Humphrey would give the poor and disenfranchised a voice," I said, repeating words that Norfleet, a Humphrey supporter, had said just that past Sunday night during his weekly phone call from college.

"That's exactly my point."

Mae joined us at the table. Then after we all bowed our heads for grace, I reminded my uncle of the terrible things that had happened in Alabama during Governor Wallace's watch—the use of tear gas and attack dogs against peaceful protesters, the mass arrests, the horrendous bombings of black churches. "I don't think that's the kind of law and order this country needs," I said.

"Wallace did what he had to do to keep his coloreds in line," Bill replied. "We're lucky that here in Edenton, *our* coloreds are civilized."

He was right about that. It seemed to me as though *everybody* in Edenton was civilized, black and white, and if there was any animosity between the races, it was politely kept inside—at least when within earshot of each other. During the years of picketing in front of the Taylor Theater, there'd been only a few arrests. Even the sit-in at Mitchener's had been peaceful. Now both facilities were legally integrated, but you'd hardly know it. The stools at the drugstore lunch counter were still mainly filled by whites. And the few blacks who ventured down from the movie theater balcony found themselves surrounded by empty seats, for the white patrons politely refused to sit anywhere near them. Even at John A. Holmes High, which had been partially integrated for nearly five years, there was little interaction between black and white students outside of class. Although laws had been passed to end segregation, customs and attitudes had stayed pretty much the same.

"The trouble with Humphrey and all those northern liberals is they want the federal government to solve our country's race problems," Bill continued. "Wallace believes that sort of thing should be left to the people." And by "the people," I knew my uncle meant "the *white* people."

Mae started clearing the dinner plates, and as our conversation shifted from politics to the delicious coconut pie she'd baked for dessert, I realized that drumming up support for Humphrey was going to be a lot harder than I'd thought. If I couldn't get my own uncle to see things my way, how was I going to convince my classmates? Mama, on the other hand, would have surely been on my side. After all, she'd been what Norfleet called a yellow-dog Democrat—one who'd vote for a yellow dog if that's who the party placed on the ticket. My great-aunt Mag had been one, too (which was one of the reasons why they got along so well). Mama's party loyalty stemmed from her gratitude to Franklin Roosevelt for getting the country through the Great Depression, but Mag's went a lot farther back. "I could never vote for a Republican," she'd once told me, "not after the way they treated the South during Reconstruction."

The funny thing is that I really wasn't all that crazy about Humphrey. I'd taken on the role of Democratic chairman because 1) nobody else at school wanted the job, 2) Norfleet, whom I considered to be an expert on just about everything, was a Humphrey supporter even though he would have preferred Eugene McCarthy or Robert Kennedy as the party's candidate, 3) Nixon, the Republican candidate, gave me the creeps, and 4) I despised George Wallace and his racist attitudes—which weren't that different from those of many Edentonians, but he acted upon them in a way I considered to be cruel and inhumane. Politics, I'd come to realize, wasn't so much about who you like as who you don't like.

As Election Day drew near, I campaigned hard at school. Then each night at dinnertime, Bill and I continued our political discussions—me urging him to support Humphrey, him steadfastly resisting, and Mae rarely saying a word because she didn't much care for argument, not even healthy debate. Then on November 5, when Wallace won by a landslide at school, I hurried home to find out how my aunt and uncle had voted at the actual polls. Maybe, just maybe, my passionate pleas had gotten through to them at the end.

"We decided to support Mr. Nixon," Mae said almost apologetically, for it wasn't customary at the time for southerners to vote Republican. And in a funny way, I felt relieved. At least they hadn't voted for Wallace.

Once the election was over, the school year seemed to fly by. Between cheerleading, my studies, and applying for college, there was little time to think about politics or race relations or even the restlessness I'd been feeling lately. High school, for better or worse, had again taken over my life—especially in late spring, when there were awards banquets, glee club concerts, and then the most anticipated event of all, Senior Prom.

With *Gone with the Wind* as the theme, the junior class transformed the gym into Tara in all her glory. The Confederate "Stars and Bars" hung above the entryway. Tall white pillars lined the dance floor. And on the back wall, behind the basketball goal, was a giant mural of a plantation house, complete with dark-skinned slaves working in the surrounding cotton fields. In keeping with the theme, I'd selected an off-white chiffon gown with a dark green sash, similar to the one Scarlett wore to the picnic at Twelve Oaks. Since I didn't have a steady boyfriend and wanted to avoid the uncertainty of waiting to be asked, I'd invited Jeff Mabe, a freckled-faced friend who'd recently moved away, to return to Edenton as my date.

The evening met all expectations—the boys looking so handsome in their rental tuxedos or white dinner jackets; the girls so elegant with our well-lacquered "up-dos," long white gloves, and corsages on our wrists. With the music of Motown playing in the background, I threw myself into the *Gone with the Wind* theme—sipping mock mint juleps, saying "fiddle-dee-dee" when my date told me I looked pretty, and swirling around the dance floor as though the belle of the ball.

When the deejay took a break, and members of the junior class performed a minstrel show, I clapped and sang along:

Oh I wish I was in the land of cotton

Old times there are not forgotten …

And I didn't consider for a moment that my five black classmates might be offended. (I don't even know if they were there.) Nor did it occur to me that glorification of a mythical Old South was what kept politicians like George Wallace going.

31. Valediction

So there I was, seated on the stage, gazing at my fellow classmates who filled the first five rows—a sea of royal-blue polyester with gold tassels hanging from mortarboards. Most of them I'd known since kindergarten, except, of course, for the five students from D. F. Walker who'd come during eighth grade as part of the district's first stage of integration. The remaining rows were filled by proud parents and grandparents, along with town dignitaries and local citizens there simply to enjoy the pomp and pageantry of a high school commencement ceremony. Mae, Bill, and Norfleet were seated in the sixth row on the left—along with Lina and George, which was unusual, because at most school functions the two sides of the family didn't mix. For a brief moment, I wished that Mama could be there with them, but I quickly shoved the thought away. *Don't go there!* I told myself. *You have a job to do.*

Though it was barely June, the temperature outside had been in the high 90s all week, and the Swain Auditorium, even with its high ceiling and electric fans, was hot and stuffy. As Mr. Holmes delivered the invocation and Words of Inspiration, I could already feel sweat forming beneath my gown and began fanning myself with my double-spaced, marked-up speech.

Being the chief cheerleader for the past two years, I was used to speaking before a large crowd and figured that delivering the valedictory address would be as easy as conducting a pep rally. Even so, while Mr. and Mrs. Leonard Ball from the Edenton Baptist Church choir sang "Sunrise, Sunset," I stopped fanning and reread my words—just to be sure they were still fresh in my mind.

It wasn't until Joey Covington, senior class president, got up to speak that the shaking began. Hardly noticeable at first, it was confined to my right foot—a simple up-down, up-down. But soon it started in my left. Then as it made its way up both legs, I placed my hands on my knees in hopes of making it stop.

When Joey finished his synopsis of senior year and introduced me as the class valedictorian, I somehow managed to stand. Then as I wobbled toward the podium and placed the crumpled speech on top, I could see that my hands were now shaking too—almost as much as my legs. A drop of sweat rolled down my forehead, and I worried that I might faint.

Clutching both sides of the podium for support, I cleared my throat and took a deep, cleansing breath, which was picked up by the microphone, causing my classmates to giggle. Then as I opened my mouth to begin, nothing came out—as though my opening words, a passage from the book of Luke, had gotten stuck somewhere between my diaphragm and throat. With sweat now steadily rolling down my cheeks, I clutched the podium tighter. And after another deep, cleansing breath (this time away from the microphone), I tried again.

"A-a-a-ask," I managed to say, sounding more donkey-like than human. I was so stunned by the strangeness of my voice that I paused for a moment to regroup. As I nervously shifted from my left foot to my right, my gold tassel swaying in front of me, I could see all seventy-seven classmates nodding their heads in unison, urging me on with their eyes.

"... and it shall be given you," I continued, my voice quivering with each syllable. "Seek and ye shall find," [pause and breathe] "knock, and it shall be opened unto you." I finished the biblical passage and trembled my way through the paragraphs on compassion and truth and putting aside our prejudices—something I truly believed in, but I was much more concerned with just getting the words out of my mouth than trying to inspire my classmates. Then, as I began the part about keeping our minds open to new ideas and opportunities, my normal speaking voice miraculously came back. Although delighted to hear it, I was so terrified that the shakiness would return that I sped through the remainder of my speech—running the words together, breathing only when necessary. When I got to the final line, "The future is ours; it can be only as bright as we make it," a collective sigh resounded throughout the auditorium.

When the ceremony ended an hour or so later, Mr. Holmes took me aside at the rear of the stage and told me I'd had a panic attack. "It was probably brought on by pent-up emotion," he said matter-of-factly.

Pent-up emotion? I had no idea what he was talking about. As far as I was concerned, there was absolutely nothing pent-up about my excitement to graduate from high school and go off to college and experience something new. I furrowed my brow to show my confusion.

"Unexpressed feelings about your mother's death," he explained. And I was suddenly angry that he'd bring up the subject on what was supposed to be a joyous occasion. Although not a trained psychologist, he'd received pastoral training in the five stages of grief—and to his way of thinking, I'd avoided or skipped through most of them. "Would you like to talk?" he'd often asked when I visited Rosemary at the rectory. "If you don't grieve now, you'll have to deal with it later." And I'd always put him off, saying "not now" or "some other time." To my way of thinking, there was absolutely nothing to be gained by wallowing in the past—whether it was Mama's death two years ago or the disastrous speech I'd just delivered.

When Principal Cecil Fry announced over the loudspeaker for all graduates to report to the school's front steps for a class photograph, I was glad for the interruption. "Sorry, I've gotta go," I said while scurrying off the stage.

In a few weeks I'd be heading to an Episcopal conference center in the Blue Ridge Mountains for a summer waitressing job—then off to Raleigh to attend St. Mary's Junior College, which at the time was a feeder school for women wanting to attend Carolina. As I'd just told the Class of 1969, there was a great, big future awaiting us. And I, for one, couldn't wait for it to begin.

The varsity cheerleading squad in front of John A. Holmes High. (I'm sixth from the left.)

My date, Jeff Mabe, and me at the prom.

Graduation night with Rosemary and her brother George. (A portrait of Mr. Holmes is in the background.)

NEW PERSPECTIVES

(1983–2012)

32. The Mama's Girl

It was something we never talked about—not when it happened, not during visits from college, and not in the decade since I'd moved north, staying in touch mainly through phone calls and letters. It wasn't because Mae was hard to talk to. In fact, she was always up for a chat. During those last two years of high school, we'd had some of our best conversations in front of the kitchen sink after dinner, her washing and me drying. "I see no point in buying a dishwasher," she liked to say. "You have to rinse off the food anyway, so you might as well clean 'em by hand."

As we'd carry out our nightly ritual, first glasses, then plates and utensils, and finally pots and pans, we'd talk about my schoolwork, the latest high school romances, the newest fashions at Belk's. We'd discuss just about anything. Anything, that is, except for the death of my mother. In the beginning, it was just too hard—we were both emotionally spent after the funeral. Then I suppose it became habit. Why bring up painful memories? I was doing just fine.

So there I was in the fall of 1983, now a mother myself, standing next to Mae at the kitchen sink as I'd done so many years before. Two-month-old Christopher was asleep in the upstairs crib, and Bill had gone outside to mow the lawn, a chore that had become recreation for him since purchasing a tractor mower soon after retirement. It was the third and final day of my visit from Boston, and at last I'd gotten to enjoy one of Mae's delicious home-cooked meals.

"We've started having our heavy meal in the middle of the day," she'd announced soon after my arrival. "It helps us keep our weight down." And although I had no complaints about the country ham sandwiches on Wonder Bread she'd made for supper that night, it wasn't the usual hearty fare I'd come to expect during visits south. I was still hungry the next morning when I awoke to the aroma of pot roast, already in the oven for the noontime meal. But then I remembered that I wouldn't be there to enjoy it.

"I'm expecting you for lunch tomorrow," my aunt Lina had said the previous evening when I stopped by to introduce her to Christopher. "Lillie's going to fry up some chicken"—which I already knew, because I'd gone into the kitchen for a glass of water and seen on the counter the package of uncooked chicken Lina's longtime maid had forgotten to refrigerate before leaving for the day.

Since George's death a few years before, Lina had become more and more dependent on Lillie. But with both of them now well into their eighties, I wondered who was taking care of whom. In the light of the noonday sun, I could see the inches of neglected dust that had accumulated on the mahogany furniture and the layers of grime on the crystal glassware. As I sat down at my aunt's well-appointed dining room table for lunch, I worried that the chicken might have begun to spoil before I rescued it the previous night. Thank goodness my uncle Jack, Lina's younger brother, would soon be moving back to Edenton to keep an eye on things.

Later that afternoon, when I returned to Mae and Bill's house to a ravenous son who'd refused to drink from a bottle while I was away, and ravenous myself from having had only a few bites of Lillie's possibly tainted fried chicken, Bill announced that he'd be treating us all to dinner that night at the Golden Corral, the buffet-style chain restaurant that had just opened across from the new shopping center a mile outside of town. "That sounds great!" I exclaimed, trying to hide my disappointment. All afternoon I'd been looking forward to leftover pot roast, and I had no desire for mediocre restaurant fare.

When we arrived at the Golden Corral at a quarter to six, I was relieved to see that the buffet counter contained a large selection of vegetables. I loaded up my tray with collards, squash, and coleslaw rather than the chicken, pork chops, and fish, which all looked the same beneath their deep-fried batters. Then, as I unloaded the individual dishes onto the table and took Christopher from my aunt's arms so she could fill her own tray, I noticed a well-dressed African-American couple entering the restaurant and approaching the buffet line. Mae caught my eye and then quickly shifted her head their way, a gesture that I took to mean either *Look how progressive Edenton has become twenty-nine years after the legal end to segregation!* or, more likely, *What is this world coming to?*

Of course I had no right to mock or judge my aunt. As Mama used to say, "People who live in glass houses shouldn't throw stones." Only a few months earlier, Paul and I had bought a house in one of Boston's most exclusive suburbs, where the only residents of color were a couple of Celtics basketball players and their families. In fact, I'd found that Boston, which was supposed to be a bastion of liberalism and tolerance, wasn't exactly what I'd expected. When I'd moved there to work right after graduating from Carolina, the city was embroiled in a busing crisis where white residents in neighborhoods like Charlestown and Southie didn't take too kindly to black children from Roxbury being assigned to their schools. As I watched it all unfold on the local news, I'd heard more words of prejudice and hate than I heard my entire childhood in Edenton. Racism, I'd quickly learned, was not just a southern thing.

When the African-American couple placed their trays on the table next to us, I could sense Mae's displeasure. "Well, it looks to me like the Golden Corral is a mighty popular place," I said cheerfully, trying to lighten the mood and avoid any comments about race. As much as I loved my aunt, I knew her prejudices were buried deep—just like my lingering grief.

The vegetables at the Golden Corral had been edible, and the soft-serve vanilla ice cream from the dispenser behind the dessert cart was refreshing. But none of it could hold a candle to what Mae prepared for me the following noon—a home-cooked feast of fried shad, fresh green beans, crookneck squash, lacy cornbread, and banana pudding for dessert. "That was the best meal I've ever eaten," I said as I unfolded the dish towel and Mae filled the sink with hot, soapy water.

Just as though there'd been no lapse in time, we resumed our well-honed ritual, her washing, me drying (still no dishwasher). We discussed the unseasonably warm October weather: "I hope Bill doesn't get overheated while he's mowing the lawn," I said.

We talked about the rising cost of groceries: "I look for specials every week in the *Chowan Herald*," said Mae. Then, as she poured the leftover grease from the cast-iron skillet into an empty Crisco can, I slowly cleared my throat. I was finally ready to bring up the subject I'd avoided far too long.

"Was Mama in a lot of pain before she died?" I began, my voice sounding thin and hollow, not quite my own. Of course I *knew* the answer, but I needed to *feel* it. The past few days, I'd revisited the scenes of my childhood, pushing Christopher in a borrowed stroller past familiar sites—St. Paul's Church, the Confederate Monument, Mitchener's Pharmacy, the house where I'd grown up. Bill had even driven me out into the country to see the now dilapidated farmhouse where Mawmaw and Granddaddy lived so many years before. As with previous trips back to Edenton, it felt strange to visit those places with so many of the people who'd made them special either dead or moved away. I occasionally saw familiar faces, but most of my high school friends (including Rosemary) were scattered far and wide. And Norfleet, now a lawyer, had a family of his own in Charlotte. Even so, the memories had flooded through me, my mother there in every scene, even when she hadn't been. I could still picture her vividly in my mind; my heart was a different matter. As hard as I tried to feel her presence and know she was looking down at her grandson and me, I couldn't—for I'd protected myself so well from her pain, I'd blocked out all her love.

When I finished asking my question, Mae just stared at the dishwater for a moment, and I began to wonder if she'd heard me. "Yes," she finally replied. "Your mama was in horrible pain, but she never complained—at least not until those last few days when her vision started to go. Not being able to read her newspapers really ticked her off."

"She couldn't see to read?" I asked in disbelief. "How could I not notice?" Even as the illness progressed, she'd buried herself in the Sunday *New York Times* and always had the latest issue of *Reader's Digest* at her bedside.

"I imagine she tried to hide it from you," Mae replied. "If I know your mama, she pretended to read just so you wouldn't worry."

"I *was* worried," I said.

"I know that."

I was silent for a moment, not quite sure what to say next. Then Mae surprised me with a snicker—not quite a laugh, but the kind of soft giggle, punctuated by a tiny snort, that was unique to her. "You know," she said, her eyes still on the sink, "Sister was still Sister, even at the very end. When the ambulance came to take her to the hospital, she took charge and told those rescue fellers exactly what to do. She knew from when your daddy died that the stretcher couldn't make it around the corners from the bedroom to the front door, so she said to 'em, 'Just take me out the back door.'"

I tried to concoct the scene in my mind, for I'd been at school at the time. "Was she spitting up blood?" I asked haltingly.

"Maybe just a little," Mae replied. Then, as if suddenly becoming aware of the gravity of my question, she added, "Nothing like your father."

Thank God.

"Your mama still had her wits about her," Mae continued. "When they carried her through the yard to get to the ambulance, she turned to me and said, as though she didn't have a care in the world, 'Aren't the azaleas beautiful this year!'"

"But she was barely conscious when I saw her in the hospital that night. It was as though she was already gone."

"They had her pretty doped up for the pain," Mae said, now reaching for a Brillo pad to scour the fish-crusted skillet, "but then the next afternoon, an hour or so before she passed, she opened her eyes for a moment and asked me, clear as a bell, to please help her make out a check and have somebody go to the bank right away to cash it. She didn't want to leave you and Norfleet without money in your pockets."

I put down my dish towel and looked at my aunt. Although she and Mama hadn't always seen eye to eye on things like fashion, home décor, and race relations, they were alike in so many ways. Mae had been at my mother's side throughout the illness and then treated me like a daughter. Mama had devoted herself to my brother and me and was still there for us at the end. If only I could be half as good a person as either of them.

"Are you okay?" Mae asked, turning from the sink and looking at me for the first time since we'd begun the conversation.

"I'm just fine," I said, struggling to hold myself together. Then I blurted out, "I miss Mama!"—sounding more like a kindergartner than a thirty-two-year-old married woman with a child of her own.

"Of course you do," Mae said. "We never stop missing our mamas. There's not a day goes by when I don't think about your grandmother."

"But I wasn't even with her when she died—I was giving tours at St. Paul's!" Tears were now rolling down my cheeks.

Mae removed her yellow rubber dishwashing gloves and gave my shoulder a squeeze. "You were doing exactly what she wanted you to do," she said. "By carrying on with your life, you were showing her you'd be okay."

"But I was so selfish toward the end," I sobbed. "A lot of the time I worried more about myself than about her."

"You were only sixteen!" Mae exclaimed. "That's what sixteen-year-olds do! Just wait until Christopher gets to be that age—you'll see."

"But did she know how much I loved her?"

"Of course she did!"

I was wiping my eyes with the dish towel when Bill appeared in the kitchen doorway, his face flushed from the warm autumn sun. "What's the matter?" he asked. "You both look like you've just lost your best friend."

"Helen's afraid she didn't show her mama enough love before she died," said Mae.

"Well, that's the silliest thing I've ever heard," Bill drawled. "You adored your mama, and she sure knew it. She used to brag that she had herself a mama's girl."

"A mama's girl?" I asked with surprise. I'd only heard of the term "mama's *boy*," and it wasn't a very flattering one.

"Yep," said Bill. "The two of you were cut from the same cloth, two peas in a pod—a regular mutual admiration society."

"And she'd be so proud if she could see you now," Mae added, "loving Christopher the way you do. She'd say she raised herself a *fine* little mama's girl."

As my aunt spoke, Bill lifted the stack of clean, dry plates from the kitchen table and carried them over to the pantry. It was well past one, almost time for *As the World Turns*, and if there was anything he'd learned during retirement, it was that Mae wouldn't want to miss even one minute of her favorite soap opera. "Don't worry about the skillet and pans," he said, shooing the two of us into the television room. "No harm in lettin' things soak a bit."

By the time the flight attendant finished her demonstration on how to fasten a seat belt, Christopher was fast asleep in my arms. Now if he could only stay that way throughout the flight back to Boston. I had a lot on my mind and didn't want to have to deal with a crying baby.

Despite what Mr. Holmes believed when I was a teenager, I'd gone through the five stages of grief long before high school graduation. I'd denied the illness. I'd bargained with God. I'd been angry and sad. It was acceptance, after all, that had propelled me to look forward, not back. But over the past few days, I'd learned that grief can't be permanently stashed away into neat little categories. Its residue is always with us—reawakened by old memories and new experiences like the birth of a child.

The previous day at Mae's kitchen sink, it had been difficult to bring up the subject of my mother's death, but also strangely cathartic. As I learned about those final days, I'd felt something shift inside of me—not just in my acknowledgment of my grief, but also in the way I remembered the past. It was subtle at first, but as I lay awake later that night, long-held childhood images of my mother began to crumble. I could identify with her pain, her courage, her concern for her children. No longer was she simply the be-all, know-all protector I'd been so afraid of losing, but rather a grown-up woman like me, with thoughts and feelings of her own.

When I stopped by Lina's house to say goodbye before leaving for the airport, I'd tried out this new perspective. I didn't sneer at the dust on the mahogany furniture. (If Lina didn't mind, why should I?) I had no derisive thoughts about my aunt's archaic master-servant relationship with Lillie. (They were lucky to have each other.) It didn't even bother me that the living room knickknacks were exactly where they'd been for decades. Instead, I thought about how for so many years Mama had come to that very house almost every Saturday night, even after Daddy's death—not because she had a particularly strong affection for her in-laws (after all, Madam and Lina had once snubbed her for being a country girl), but because she believed it was important to maintain family ties for my brother and me. Wasn't I doing the same for Christopher?

"Hope you'll come back to see me again soon," Lina said when we parted.

"Sure thing!" I'd replied—not because I *wanted* to return, but because I knew that I would.

As I replayed the scene in my mind, I peered out the airplane window and tried to imagine my mother's spirit floating above the clouds and praising me for my newfound maturity. But all I saw was the glare of my own reflection in the glass. Bill *had* said the previous day that Mama and I were cut from the same cloth, two peas in a pod. Maybe seeing myself instead of her was proof. If I really thought about it, Mama and I weren't all that different in temperament—both of us bossy, opinionated, and often impatient. But what about her more positive traits? Had I inherited any of them as well?

She left the farm for town, but never forgot her roots.

She was raised with the mentality of the Jim Crow South, but was willing to open her mind.

She appreciated the beauty of a warm spring day, even at her darkest hour.

She always loved her children.

I looked down at Christopher and smiled. And deep inside, I somehow knew that my mother was smiling too.

33. The Expatriated Southerner

Travel from Boston to Edenton became an annual family event. As Christopher and his younger sister, Ginny, got older, they looked forward to spending February or April school breaks in North Carolina, where under the warmth of the southern sun they'd fish in the creek behind Mae and Bill's house, climb on the Revolutionary War cannons that overlooked the bay, and hunt along the shore for buried treasure left by the pirates who once navigated the Albemarle Sound waters. As far as they were concerned, Edenton was a parklike paradise where children could run free and let their imaginations go wild.

As for me, I considered those yearly trips to be tours of duty more than pleasure travel. Of course, I enjoyed spending time with Mae and Bill, who treated Chris and Ginny like their own grandchildren. I also enjoyed having a break from New England's raw winters or unpredictable springs. But Edenton represented two things I'd tried so hard to leave behind me when I moved to

Massachusetts: grief over my mother's death and shame for the racial system I'd grown up with. After the birth of Christopher, I'd learned to manage my feelings of loss. Now, eight years later, I was still grappling with the issue of race. My new job with the Weston Public Schools was helping.

"So why do you want the job?" asked Mr. Anthony Bryant as he took a seat across from me in the school office. Dressed in a collared shirt and slacks, he appeared much less imposing than the dark, heavy-set, dashiki-clad man who'd bellowed out the seven principles of *Nguzo Saba* at a Kwanzaa ceremony nearly four months earlier. Even so, there was something in his demeanor that made me squirm—not quite hostility, but an aura of distrust that made me wonder whether he had something against me personally or it was the way he felt about white people in general. I'd just been interviewed by the Weston School District's coordinator of METCO, a state-funded, voluntary desegregation program in which inner-city children of color were bused to the area's predominantly white suburban schools. Now it was Mr. Bryant's turn to see if I was someone that he and the other Boston parents could work with.

When my prospective boss, Mrs. McCullough, told me that the head of the African-American parents' group would be stopping by her office to chat with me, I'd thought it was just a perfunctory part of the interview process. After all, I'd been highly recommended for the job by the district's retiring community liaison because of what she referred to as my "outstanding work as a parent volunteer." Since kindergarten, both of my children (Chris, age eight, and Ginny, a year and a half younger) had been part of METCO Family Friends, a program that encouraged resident students to socialize with their urban classmates outside the classroom. "You're a shoo-in!" the retiring community liaison had told me. "All you have to do is fill out the application." But now, left alone in the office with Mr. Bryant, I wasn't quite so sure. He didn't seem like the kind of man who was easily swayed by recommendations.

"Why do I want the job?" I said slowly, repeating the question in order to buy more time for the right answer. Of course there were practical reasons for wanting to work for my children's school district. After eight years as a stay-at-home mom, I was eager to return to the workplace—and with hours that mostly coincided with Chris and Ginny's school day, there'd be no need for childcare. As a parent volunteer, I'd enjoyed attending the program's potlucks, field trips, parent discussions, and Kwanzaa celebrations. Why not get paid for organizing them?

"I want the job because I believe in educational opportunity for all children," I replied, thinking it was the answer Mr. Bryant would want to hear. After all, the METCO program, which had been established in the 1960s as a remedy for the racial inequities within the Boston public school system, was an acronym for Metropolitan Council for Educational Opportunity. As I spoke, I tried to conceal any traces of a drawl because during my nineteen years in the Boston area, I'd learned that northerners often had preconceived notions about white southerners.

"Educational opportunity for all children," he repeated skeptically, perhaps wondering why I'd given him such an obvious answer. And I suddenly wished that I'd told him the whole truth—that my desire to be part of METCO had as much to do with myself and my own children as the students being bused from the inner city for a good education.

When I moved to New England to work after college, I'd wanted to separate myself from the South. As far as I was concerned, I wasn't a typical white southerner. I'd read *Soul on Ice* by Eldridge Cleaver and the poetry of Maya Angelou. I'd cast my first presidential ballot for George McGovern. Why not live in a place that better suited me ideologically? So I settled down among people like me in the suburbs west of Boston, where far removed from the struggles of those living in the inner city, we'd denounce racism and discrimination (if the subjects ever came up in conversation) yet live our lives within a comfortable bubble of whiteness.

Then Chris and Ginny were born, and I worried about raising them amid so much whiteness. My childhood was limited by Jim Crow and its aftermath, theirs by demographics. If our children were to grow up with an appreciation of diversity, Paul and I knew that having them watch *Sesame Street* and read multicultural picture books wouldn't be enough. As soon as they were old enough to enter Weston's public schools, our family got involved with METCO.

"By *all* children," I said, trying to amend my previous answer, "I mean suburban kids, too." Then as I explained my real reasons for wanting the job, I realized that my initial assessment of Mr. Bryant had been wrong. He was attentive. He asked questions. What I had perceived earlier as distrust was actually a desire to get to know me and to hire a community liaison who was passionate about the METCO program. I told him about my segregated education in the South. He told me about his in the North. We realized that despite our different backgrounds, we had much in common. We both valued diversity. We both wanted our children to get a good education. By the time Mrs. McCullough returned to her office to signal the end of the interview, we knew we could work together.

"Is Mae a racist?" Chris asked a few weeks later during our annual family trip to Edenton. Although I'd asked myself the same thing many times in the past, I was surprised by his question. From what I could tell, Mae rarely offered opinions about race when around the children, and she no longer used the "n-word" in everyday conversation. Had he noticed that she wasn't very interested in my new job? Or maybe he'd overheard her telling me that she and my uncle had tried to get the right of first refusal on their neighbors' property in case it ever went on the market because, as she put it, "We don't want to end up living next to coloreds."

"Mae doesn't *hate* black people," I told my son. "She just grew up during a time when many whites believed that blacks were inferior to them. We now know that such thinking was wrong—but some people, like Mae, have had a hard time letting go of the ideas of the past."

I wasn't trying to make excuses for my aunt. I just wanted Chris to understand that race is a very complex issue. He'd learned about the civil rights movement through Black History Month school assemblies and METCO activities. He had African-American friends. Even so, I knew it would be so easy for him to draw simplistic conclusions—to see history through the stereotypes of mean-spirited, oppressive whites and victimized blacks, or to assume that the struggle for racial equality had been achieved with civil rights legislation. Using Mae as an example, I wanted him to know that racial equality, in attitude as well as action, is still a work in progress.

Later that morning, when I saw a sign at the foot of Edenton's Broad Street advertising a "Town-wide Gospel Sing-along," I thought it would be a great opportunity to show my children the positive changes that had taken place in Edenton during the past couple of decades. I envisioned blacks and whites from the town's various churches getting together to sing old gospel favorites like "He's Got the Whole World in His Hands" and "Down by the Riverside." Ginny and Chris would be able to experience interracial community spirit and see the New South at its best.

Mae and Bill weren't very enthusiastic when I told them about the sing-along. "Is it black gospel or white gospel?" Mae asked. (I hadn't considered that there was a difference.) Paul, who wasn't particularly fond of gospel music of any kind, decided that he'd prefer spending his Sunday afternoon reading. But Chris and Ginny, who were always up for an outing, thought it would be fun to attend an event at the Swain Auditorium, the place where I'd received my high school diploma many years before.

We arrived a little bit late, and it wasn't until we'd taken our seats in the back of the old, musty auditorium that I realized Mae was right about there being a difference between black and white gospel. Everyone in the audience was white. When I looked down at my program and read that the event was being sponsored by one of the town's all-white evangelical churches, I cringed—for I equated southern evangelicalism with the anti-science, anti-choice, anti-union, anti-immigrant, anti–affirmative action, anti-gay, pro-gun, right-wing politics that went completely against my grain.

My first thought was to get up and leave. This was clearly not going to be the interracial, interdenominational event I'd anticipated. But then I remembered a conversation I'd had with my brother shortly after Dukakis lost the last presidential election. Norfleet (still somewhat liberal, at least by southern standards) had said that one of the reasons for the drubbing was that northern Democrats had a condescending and dismissive attitude toward southern religion. "You need to be more open-minded," he'd told me, "and try to show a little respect." Even as an adult, I took my big brother's words to heart, so as I settled into my creaky wooden seat, I tried hard to follow his advice. When two African-American women in Sunday church hats entered the auditorium and joined us in the back row, I began to feel a little better.

The teenage band that accompanied the sing-along was pretty good. And while the Christian rock repertoire didn't include the familiar Mahalia Jackson–style gospel songs I'd hoped for, the tunes were catchy enough that I was able to hum along. I was actually enjoying myself. But then the preaching began, and I couldn't help but cringe again. As the young, charismatic pastor railed against Satan and spoke of the heavenly rewards awaiting those who sought salvation, I began to wonder if it was evangelical dogma, more than politics, that went against my grain.

I'd been brought up as an Episcopalian, which my non-Episcopalian friends used to call the "anything goes" denomination. Drinking, cursing, and dancing with gyrating hips were fine—as long as done in moderation. Scripture was not taken literally, but used for inspiration and moral guidance. In Sunday school, I was encouraged to question, even to doubt, as I explored my own spirituality. In contrast, the evangelicals before me seemed to possess a certainty, almost a smugness, that those who believe as they do and follow the rules of their faith would be guaranteed a spot in heaven.

While no expert on religion, I was of the opinion that too much certainty bordered on self-righteousness and that too much rigidity kept people from thinking for themselves. As the pastor implored the children in the audience to obey their parents, citing Ephesians 6:1, I thought about how Mama had imposed few rules on my brother and me. She'd insisted, however, that we be kind, honest, and fair. "Just do the right thing," she'd often said, without explicitly telling us what that might be. (She wanted us to figure it out.) Then if we acted in a way that wasn't kind, honest, or fair, she'd express her disappointment with a scolding and ask how what we'd done "sat" with us. (Usually not very well.)

She also had a way of asking us questions that made us think beyond ourselves—like the first day of integration at John A. Holmes High when I told her it was no big deal since none of the black students had been assigned to my college-prep classes. "Maybe not for you," she'd replied. "But don't you imagine it was a pretty big deal for the kids who were brave enough to transfer to a white school?" Then there was the time I joked about the substitute teacher, Mrs. Browning, falling asleep during class. "Do you think she meant to fall asleep?" Mama asked. "Have you considered that she might have a health condition?" Although opinionated like me, Mama was never unkind or judgmental. If she were there with me at the sing-along, I doubt she'd be cringing at the evangelicals for their politics and religion. Instead, she'd be trying to understand why they think and believe as they do.

When the preaching finally ended, the rock band started up again, and the audience rose to its feet with hands lifted toward the heavens. Then as shouts of *Praise-the-Lord* filled the auditorium, the pastor, with quivering voice, invited all doubters and nonbelievers to come forward and accept Jesus Christ as Lord and Savior. That was when the two African-American ladies in Sunday church hats got up and left the auditorium.

"Can we leave, too?" Chris whispered, and I could see in both his and Ginny's faces their discomfort with the mounting religious fervor. (Until that afternoon, their only experience with organized religion had been at Weston's Unitarian church, where services tended to be more cerebral than emotional.)

"Yes, it's time to go," I replied, not just referring to the sing-along. Despite my uneasiness that afternoon, there was much I still loved about Edenton and the South. I cherished the ties to family, the rural landscapes, the warmth of the people and the climate. But I'd built a new life for myself in Massachusetts, a life that I'd be returning to the following day with the people I cared about most. I was already picturing the shimmering Boston skyline as the flight from Norfolk approached Logan, and then arriving at our cozy, tan Cape amid the oaks and firs of Weston.

For better or worse, the South would always be a part of me. My roots were in its soil. It held a piece of my heart. But as I clasped my children's soft, pink hands and quietly exited the auditorium, I knew it was no longer home.

In Edenton with Norfleet, 2009.

34. Inevitabilities

In the spring of 1957, the Honorable William S. Privott of the Chowan County Superior Court announced that it was the first time since 1869 that the courts had convened without a man named Pruden being a member of the County Bar. After citing the contributions of my great-grandfather, W. D. Pruden, my grandfather, James Norfleet Pruden, Sr., and those of my recently deceased father, he said that he hoped James Norfleet Pruden III, then age eight, would "feel an urgent call to enter the legal profession and thus continue to carry on the outstanding record of the Pruden Family."

Sixteen years later, with a B.A. from Carolina and a law degree from the University of Virginia, my brother, Norfleet, began a distinguished career at a Charlotte law firm and later served as president of the North Carolina Bar Association, as our great-grandfather had done nearly a century before. It was inevitable. He'd had a calling. And I often envied his seemingly predetermined path through life.

My own journey has been much more circuitous. Unlike Norfleet, I hopped from one job to the next—some I hated (waitressing and secretarial work) and others I enjoyed (advertising account executive, community liaison for METCO, and writing/editorial work in California). Unlike Norfleet, who met the love of his life on a college blind date and started a family right after law school, I dated many men over the years before discovering love and the joys of parenthood in my thirties. And unlike Norfleet, who established firm roots in Charlotte, I've called many places home—five Boston-area communities, the Bay Area of California, and most recently San Diego.

But even with all those twists and turns and pleasant surprises, I've carried with me my own sense of inevitability—not a calling or clear vision of the future as Norfleet seemed to have, but rather a deep-seeded presentiment that sometimes filled me with worry and dread. I believed that I'd one day get breast cancer like my mother.

Since beginning annual mammograms at age thirty-five, my reaction to the procedure was always the same. That knot in the stomach before picking up the phone to make the appointment. The rapid heartbeat while pretending to read eight-month-old *Newsweeks* in the medical center's waiting area. The shortness of breath on the way to the changing room. ("Please strip to the waist; the gown opens in front.") And then afterward, the waiting period, when my mind would race with my own worst fears and memories of what my mother went through—the discovery of a tumor, the spread of the disease into the liver, the leaving behind of two children.

During the early years, the waiting usually ended quickly—twenty minutes or so alone in front of a video on self-examination until the technician interrupted to say, "Everything's fine. Come back in a year." But as the precision of mammography expanded, so did my agony. "We'll call you in a couple of days if there are concerns," I'd be told. "Otherwise you'll get a report in the mail."

So I'd carry my anxieties home with me—panicking whenever the phone rang, for fear that it was the radiology department calling with bad news, checking the mailbox each day for a letter saying I was okay. There were a few times over the years when the results were inconclusive and I'd be called back for more tests. "With your family history," I'd be told, "we recommend an ultrasound." And when the results came back negative, I'd feel joy and relief. At least for the next eleven months or so, I wouldn't have to think about inevitability.

It was during the summer after turning sixty when I noticed a tautness in my right breast. *Nothing to be concerned about*, I told myself. My previous mammogram had shown nothing. I could feel no lump. Maybe I'd overworked a pectoral muscle while playing tennis.

But the radiation technician seemed worried when I went in for my annual mammogram that fall. "Your right breast doesn't look normal," she said before beginning the procedure. "I'll be recommending further tests regardless of what your films show." *An overly zealous technician*, I told myself. But deep inside, I feared the worst.

Two agonizing weeks later—after undergoing a compression mammogram and ultrasound (both inconclusive) followed by an MRI and needle biopsy—I received the diagnosis: invasive ductile carcinoma, stage III.

Yes, I'd developed breast cancer like my mother. But that's as far as I'll allow inevitability to go. When Mama was diagnosed forty-six years ago, her only treatment options were radical mastectomy, radiation, and then hoping for the best. Chemotherapy was not yet readily available, and targeted treatments based on estrogen, progesterone, or HER2 receptors had not been developed. There were no breast cancer support groups or three-day walks for a cure. The disease was rarely discussed in polite company—partly because female anatomy was involved, but also because a breast cancer diagnosis at the time was considered by most to be a death sentence.

I, on the other hand, am of a different place and time. I live only five miles from Scripps Clinic, a world-renowned medical center where a team of well-trained specialists was able to use the latest scientific research to treat my specific case. I was given six rounds of neo-adjuvant chemotherapy, which shrank my tumor from eight centimeters to less than two. I've undergone surgery and radiation. For the next five years, I'll be taking estrogen-blocking medication to prevent a recurrence. My prognosis is good.

Unlike my mother, I've lived to see both of my children graduate from high school and college. I've been there to guide them through the ups and downs of young adulthood. I've seen them develop into caring, productive adults. If they marry, I intend to dance at their weddings. If they have babies, I intend to hold my grandchildren.

I suppose I'm still a bit like the Confederate soldier at the foot of Edenton's Broad Street: I don't give in easily to defeat. I intend to survive this disease. And with the grace of God and good medical care, I will.

Acknowledgements

Thanks to the many friends and fellow writers who read my manuscript at various stages and offered valuable feedback; to author and writing coach Lisa Fugard, who helped me become a better writer; to Lisa Wolff for her superb copyediting skills; to Jeniffer Thompson and the good people at MonkeyCMedia for giving my book a professional look; to fellow Edenton native Carroll Lassiter, who allowed me to use one of her exquisite paintings on the cover; to Karla Olson for guiding me through the ins and outs of quality self-publishing; and most of all, to my husband, Paul, for his steadfast love and support.

READING GROUP DISCUSSION QUESTIONS:

1. What is the significance of the title, *White Gloves and Collards*?
2. The Confederate monument at the foot of Edenton's Broad Street is fraught with symbolism. What did it mean to young Helen? Are there other symbols of the Old South in the book?
3. Political and social events such as the Greensboro sit-ins and the assassinations of President Kennedy and Dr. Martin Luther King, Jr. play a role in the author's emerging view of the world. How were you or your parents personally affected by those events?
4. In chapter 33, the author laments that her childhood relationships were limited by Jim Crow and its aftermath. How so? In what ways has your own life experience been affected by social barriers?
5. Young Helen observes class differences within her extended family. Why do you think she has an affinity for her mother's side?

6. In chapter 30, the author describes the civility between the races in Edenton. Do you think that the town's culture of politeness inhibited social change or facilitated it?
7. The author compares her community's fear of integration to hurricanes that make their way across the Albemarle Sound. How has your own community handled social change over the years?
8. Based on young Helen's observations of her own mother, what were some of the challenges of being a single mother during the 1950s and early 1960s? In what ways is it easier or more difficult today?
9. Beginning with the death of her father, young Helen endures a series of losses. How do age and maturity affect her handling of those tragedies?
10. After the birth of her son, the adult Helen's image of her mother begins to change. How have your perspectives of your own parents changed over time?
11. In chapter 9, young Helen notes that unlike her brother, who was born with a sense of fairness, it was something she'd have to learn. In what ways did Norfleet and Mama teach her? Do you believe that fairness is an innate quality?
12. Rather than a continuous narrative, the author uses vignettes and stories about her family to describe her childhood. What has been the role of storytelling in your own family history?

RECIPES

Mawmaw's Collards

If she were alive today, my grandmother would probably be amused by the rising status of green leafy vegetables like kale, turnip greens, and collards. Once a staple for poor whites and African-Americans in the rural South, collards can now be found on the menus of some of the finest restaurants. While Mawmaw used a woodstove and cooked her collards for hours, modern cook tops and less cook time will work just fine.

Ingredients:

- Desired amount of collards
- Ham hock or slab of fatback
- Salt and pepper to taste
- Vinegar

Thoroughly wash the collard leaves and tear into medium-size pieces. Discard the thick center ribs. Place the ham hock or fatback in a large pot of boiling water and simmer for up to an hour. Remove the meat, turn down the heat, and add the collards. Cook until desired doneness. Drain. Season with salt, pepper, and a little bit of vinegar.

Lucy's Fried Chicken

According to Lucy Lamb, who worked for my family during my mother's illness, there are two secrets to good fried chicken: soaking the chicken beforehand in salt water or buttermilk and keeping the oil hot. In my few attempts to replicate this recipe, my greatest challenge has been to cook the chicken until done without burning the crust. One solution is to fry the meat until crispy, place on a wire rack over a cookie sheet, and then finish cooking in the oven (15 to 20 minutes at 400 degrees F).

Ingredients:

- Chicken parts
- Salt water or buttermilk for soaking
- Flour seasoned with salt, pepper, and paprika
- Crisco

After washing and trimming the chicken pieces, place in a bowl of salt water or buttermilk and refrigerate for 6 to 12 hours. When ready to cook, coat the drained chicken in seasoned flour. Melt enough Crisco to fill one-third of a cast-iron skillet. When hot, add chicken pieces and fry until done (10 to 15 minutes per side).

Lillie's Corn Pudding

When Lillie Usher began working for my grandmother Madam in the early 1900s, refrigerators were not yet common household appliances, so many families used evaporated milk rather than fresh dairy products for both drinking and cooking. In this recipe, the evaporated milk can be replaced with cream, but I think that the canned milk makes for a better consistency.

Ingredients:

2 cups white corn (canned, frozen, or fresh)
½ cup flour
1 small can evaporated milk
2 eggs, beaten
½ cup sugar
½ stick melted butter
Pinch of salt
Dash of vanilla

Preheat oven to 350 degrees F. In a large mixing bowl, beat all ingredients together thoroughly, and cook in a buttered casserole for 45 minutes.

Mae's Sock-It-To-Me Poundcake

During the late 1960s, when Mae clipped this recipe from Edenton's weekly paper, The Chowan Herald, *"Sock it to me!" was a popular catchphrase from the hit TV series* Rowan and Martin's Laugh-In. *My aunt often served this cake for dessert, but it's also a great brunch coffeecake.*

Ingredients:

1 package yellow cake mix
1 cup sour cream
½ cup vegetable oil
¼ cup sugar
¼ cup water
4 eggs
Filling: 1 cup chopped pecans, 2 tablespoons brown sugar, and 2 teaspoons cinnamon
Glaze: 1 cup confectioners' sugar and 2 tablespoons milk

Preheat oven to 375 degrees F. In a large mixing bowl, blend the cake mix, sour cream, oil, sugar, water, and eggs. Beat with a mixer for two minutes. Pour half of the batter into a greased and floured 10-inch tube pan. Sprinkle with the filling and add the rest of the batter. Bake for 25 minutes. Cool for 10 minutes and remove from pan. For the glaze, mix together the confectioner's sugar and milk, and drizzle over cake.

CPSIA information can be obtained at www.ICGtesting.com
Printed in the USA
BVOW07s0135080914

365721BV00001B/32/P

9 780989 801102